PRAISE FOR *QUICKSAND*

In *Quicksand*, Jennifer Riegler salutes unsung heroes that others would pass by without even seeing. Her lyrical prose and poignant poetry highlight these heroes and open our eyes to see these courageous ones in their true light. This book will challenge you to step out of your ordinary life and into an extraordinary life, walking on quicksand sometimes but helping others in an amazing way.

Patricia Foster

Patricia Foster is an author and veteran missionary with TEAM — The Evangelical Alliance Mission.

QUICKSAND

Stories of Gemstones
Who Rebuild What Is Broken

Jennifer Riegler

Published by
Innovo Publishing LLC
www.innovopublishing.com
1-888-546-2111

Providing Full-Service Publishing Services for
Christian Authors, Artists, and Organizations: Hardbacks, Paperbacks,
eBooks, Audiobooks, Music, and Film

QUICKSAND
Stories of Gemstones Who Rebuild What Is Broken

ISBN 13: 978-1-61314-257-8

Interior Layout by Innovo Publishing LLC
Illustrations by Aditya Jhunjhunwala
Cover Design by Deepak Peters

Printed in the United States of America
U.S. Printing History
First Edition: February 2015

DEDICATION

They will sparkle in His land like jewels in a crown.
Zechariah 9:16

Afflicted city, lashed by storms and not comforted,
I will rebuild you with stones of turquoise,
your foundations with lapis lazuli.

I will make your battlements of rubies,
your gates of sparkling jewels,
and all your walls of precious stones.

All your children will be taught by the Lord,
and great will be their peace.

Isaiah 54:11–13

Quicksand is dedicated to those who rebuild what is broken,
who do it silently, every day of their lives.
They are God's precious gemstones.

TO PONDER

Never choose to be a worker, but when once God has put His call on you, woe be to you if you turn to the right hand or to the left. God will do with you what He never did with you before the call came; He will do with you what He is not doing with other people. Let Him have His way.

Oswald Chambers, *The Complete Works of Oswald Chambers*

AUTHOR'S NOTE

These life stories in *Quicksand* are based on my experiences. Names have been changed, characters combined, and events compressed. Certain episodes are imaginative re-creations, and those episodes are not intended to portray actual events.

I am so excited and thankful that you have chosen to be a part of my journey. As you read through these life stories and meet my unsung heroes, I believe your spirit will be stirred up, even as your heart breaks. May *Quicksand* inspire you and bless you in a significant way.

CONTENTS

PREFACE

QUICKSAND

Kevin Spacey blurts out smirkily in the film *American Beauty*, "Nope. I'm just an ordinary guy with nothing to lose." That line stirred me. It was 1999. It stayed with me, and I drifted way beyond the context of the film and Kevin Spacey.

Most of us consider ourselves ordinary, but we do have something to lose. We may come from modest backgrounds, lead simple lives, but all that we do is of worth. It impacts the people we connect with, beginning with our family, extending to our neighborhood, and stretching right up to that person we bump into on a holiday or a bus ride.

I have had the privilege of crossing paths with some precious people who live each day in that awareness. They believe that we are summoned onto planet Earth for a unique purpose—a purpose crafted out just for them, one only they can fulfill. They hear the Call; they walk on quicksand, and their lives become extraordinary.

Quicksand is about the simple things, the real things. It is about the men and women who do things. They distill the noise, hear the melody, learn the lessons, and pay the price. I salute them. Let me tell you the story of my gemstones. I encourage you to find your own gems, to write your own story as you dip into *Quicksand*.

May *Quicksand* ignite the extraordinary in you, and may this planet be blessed with true and simple men and women doing things that pay rich tribute to the God of this universe, Whom I have come to love and know as my Father.

GEMSTONES

Have you ever been called a gem? Did someone ever make you feel like one? Have you ever eaten one at least?

My first exposure to the word *gem* was when I was a little girl, perhaps six or seven years old. We had these lovely little button chocolates called Cadbury Gems, and they came in varied colors, identical in shape but so colorful. Each one in the pack seemed to have a personality of its own. They are similar to M&Ms. I remember spending a lot of time arranging these precious gems in different patterns, then choosing and sorting them in a certain order based on how close I felt to a certain color that day. There was no logic to it. They were playful, lovely gems. I would put one in my mouth and chew on it, pull it out, and look at its colorless form, and suddenly the gem looked so unappealing! Whatever happened to it? It would go right back into my mouth again, and the chocolate bit inside somehow didn't make up for its loss of color.

As the years rolled on, the word *gem* began to mean more than just colorful, chocolate-filled buttons. In 2010, I came upon a small city in India where I had close encounters with gemstones. Real ones, not chocolates. I saw them in all shapes, sizes, colors, and sparkles, dazzling and brilliant. Each seemed to have a hidden beauty of its own, much beyond what the visible eye could see. Some very polished, some rough on the edges — each one was a gem.

I wanted to know more about them. So I went seeking and learning. It was heady. Too much information about the refractive index, dispersion, specific gravity, hardness, cleavage, fracture, luster, luminescence, and absorption spectrum. But what bedazzled me most of all was a much understated line: *Material or flaws within a stone may be present as inclusions.*

God's creation is flawless. You, me, the animals, mountains, valleys, rivers, and the seas were perfectly handcrafted by the Creator, and our flaws are part of us. They are to be seen as inclusions. They give us our personality and make us unique.

PART 1: TIGER EYE

TIGER EYE

Have you met a tiger in the eye?
Have you felt his breath so close?
Did you whisper a speechless nothing?
Did you promise yourself something?
Were you just so shaken by his fierce wild?
Or were you broken by his grace . . .

Here is the story of a man whose fierce and
passionate relationship with God, led him to do
things that are truly extraordinary.
He is my tiger eye.

AND IT WAS MORNING

Mordechai woke up to the familiar morning sounds outside his window. The sparrows and the parrots were chatting with each other. They were talking loud and clear in the language of the angels, perhaps sharing their dreams and nightmares. Mordechai believed they were singing and praising God for the new day, the sunshine, and the promise of life. It was 6:00 a.m. and the air was full of the pledge of a new dawn. The sun would be up soon. He stood by the window breathing in the only bit of fresh air that he knew he would receive all day, yet his heart held anticipation. He never stopped believing.

His small room wasn't much to talk about. But it was home, and the view of golden, powerful, dazzling rays of sunshine that reflected on the high-rise buildings each morning was always special. His heart captured images that his mind could not decipher. The one single emotion that overpowered his senses during those moments was joy, and that was enough. Those morning moments were simply perfect.

Mordechai's room was in the middle of a large slum in the suburbs of Mumbai. It was an all-in-one living room-bedroom-kitchen. There were a few common toilets outside the slum. Although it was a slum, the dwellers here were very conscientious about their hygiene and health. It was a clean slum, one among the few real clean ones in this city of millions. Mordechai had good neighbors. They were family to each other. They shared food and daily chores, like filling water into buckets from the community taps at the end of the slum. The older ones took care of children when parents were at work. It was a delightful little community.

Mordechai went about his morning, had his breakfast, got ready for the day, and stepped out to work. He was twenty-eight years old. He had been living in Mumbai since he left home and landed on the Victoria Terminus train junction a few years ago. A little village in rural Orissa, which is in the east of India, lays claim to Mordechai's childhood. He makes annual pilgrimages to his little village to stay connected with his childhood and the fragile remnants of his family.

IT WASN'T JUST ANOTHER DAY

He was walking his usual path to the office one Tuesday morning, after doing the dreaded rail route, but Mordechai didn't make it to his office. On the curb around the corner, lay a pile of grime. The grime seemed to move a bit. As our young man got closer, the grime almost seemed human. Could it be? What was going on? Mordechai came closer and, bending over the grime, he took a closer look. It was a man indeed, clothed in grime and soot. He was sick.

Mordechai was numb. He felt compelled by the situation. His thoughts seemed like a crazy cacophony of words and emotions bursting all at once, through the corridors of his mind. Clearly the man needed a doctor. He needed to be in a hospital, and he needed an ambulance to get there. He seemed to be in need of everything!

Most of all, he needed a bed to lie on to die a peaceful death. Our grimy man was on his way to rest forever. A normal day had suddenly turned into a momentous one.

Mordechai swooped up the man in his arms and let him breathe his last few breaths in a warm and silent embrace. His strong, young arms held a trembling, shriveled up, dying man, and in those few moments that elapsed between life and death, Mordechai decided to spend his day differently. He went about planning a dignified last rite for the dead man. After a lot of here and there, digging and searching, Mordechai found himself in a small hut made of bricks and blue plastic sheets. The dead man had lived here. A teeny brown-eyed boy was at play with his few possessions, very oblivious and unaware that a few moments ago his life had changed dramatically—the only person who was family to him had left him forever.

THE DAYS AFTER

Mordechai kept gazing at the child, and the child did not repel his company. They held hands in silent agreement and walked out of the door. Night fell over the city. Mordechai made a meal of noodles and egg for the two of them. They ate together and in doing so, they sealed their friendship as well. Morning came and the familiar rays of the sun went unnoticed. Everything had changed for both of them. The child's name was Moses, and he was four years old.

Mordechai kept watching little Moses who had made himself at home in Mordechai's small room. He was a child of very few words. His large, dark brown eyes did most of the talking. Moses knew that something was not right. His dad had not turned up at home many nights before. Aunty Sheila next door had taken care of him on such nights, but this time Moses knew that something was wrong; it seemed like Daddy wasn't coming back. Mordechai looked away for a few moments and then went up to Moses, took him onto his lap in a back embrace, and the tears rolled on the ground. Mordechai kept rocking Moses on his lap, and they cried silently together.

Moses now lived with Mordechai. It had been three months since the death of his father. Moses had soaked himself into the very fabric of Mordechai's life. Mordechai went to work reluctantly each morning, leaving Moses to the observing and caring eyes of Hannah. Hannah was sixty years old and lived next door. She knew Mordechai as she would her very own son.

Have you ever heard of memory spots? Well, you may have a different term for them. Memory spots are places, incidents, or people that have left behind something tangible. When I am on a memory spot, I am reliving that incident or experience all over again. Mordechai had one of his memory spots each day now on his way to work. Yes, it was the place where he had held the dying man in his arms. Each morning as Mordechai came close to the spot, he felt like he would choke, and he found it difficult to breathe. He felt strange things, feelings he could not recognize nor articulate. It could best be defined as a calling, a beckoning. One fine morning Mordechai decided to listen.

THE CALL

Are you aware of the Bible stories?
Heard of them being called?
Abraham, Moses, Jacob,
Elijah, Nehemiah, Esther,
David, John, and Peter.

They were called to leave the familiar
and go with Him on an adventure.
To break, to build, to change, to lead.
They pled, they bled, and yet cleaved
to the Call that was so deep.

Many are called to this day
by the Ancient of Days.
Thrilling journeys await those
who dare to leave, new things to cleave.

THE TRANSFORMATION

Mordechai heard the Call. He heard it in the beat of his heart; he felt it in the sweat on his back, in the trembling in his legs. He felt it in his breath. It was the Fourth of July. While Americans on the other side of the planet celebrated their independence day and their right to happiness, Mordechai walked with his head bent down deep in thought and stepped into his boss's cabin. Announcing his resignation, he relinquished his right to himself to follow God's leading. He surrendered his future to God and went back home to Moses.

As Mordechai walked down the street to his room, he didn't seem to notice the hard drops of rain that kept pelting him. It was windy; the trees were moaning and groaning as they tried to hold their trunks straight and fight the wind. Mordechai saw nothing. He only heard a loud drum beat in his heart. He desired to be with Moses. He wanted to take care of him and be a father to him. In the days that followed, he watched and interacted with Moses intently. He wanted to know him. Moses was just learning to converse then. Moses was precious; he was a gift. He was the beginning of Mordechai's transformation.

Arising from the half-broken chair that he sat on, Mordechai dropped Moses in the caring arms of Hannah and stepped outside. He walked. In those few hours he journeyed through the quicksand of his life. Flashes of the past, the present, and the uncertain future all seemed to flow in varied patterns and colors like a sand blow. Every now and then he felt the force of gravity pulling him downward. But another stronger force kept pulling him up.

Mordechai had reached the edge of a forest—the only one of its kind in the city—and as he walked through it, he felt a kind of lightness like that of soap bubbles flying aimlessly in the backdrop of a clear, blue sky. He looked at the expanse of greenery ahead of him and promised the forest that he would be back another time. Tracing back his steps to the nearest police station, he registered Moses's existence.

Moses became Mordechai's first son, one among the many he would adopt over the coming years. Moses went to kindergarten and started speaking in English to the delight of his neighbors, who were not so well versed with the language. The entire neighborhood had heard of Moses and their hearts warmed up to him instantly.

Mordechai had quit his job as you know. His days began with the first glorious moments of sunshine and breakfast with Moses. As they prepared themselves for the day, they would hold hands together and Mordechai would whisper a prayer to the God of his Bible. Mordechai would then drop Moses off at his school and live the rest of the day in real-life adventures, working hard to rescue other street children like Moses.

It's been fifteen years to that day since Mordechai rescued and adopted little Moses. Moses is nineteen years old now. He plays the guitar and works as a technician. He will marry someday, have children of his own, and write his own story. But let us journey back to the beginning when Mordechai rescued other street boys like Moses and set up a home for them.

Mordechai lived each day to rescue abandoned street children. His first daily trip would be to the big railway station he was so familiar with. He had been in and out of it every day before. But now he saw things at this station that he had never noticed. He quietly observed a band of boys who worked and begged on the varied platforms of this station. They would huddle together in groups every now and then, whisper things, share some food they had found or begged for, and then quickly disperse to their regular spots as they saw a train pull in.

Over a couple of months, Mordechai managed to make his presence felt, and the band grew quite fond of him. They met once a week. Mordechai would always get them something to eat, some clothes to wear, and he would spend time getting to know them—hearing their dreadful stories, wiping their tears, and cracking jokes with them. But it took some time to make friends with them, to win their hearts, and it took the boys much longer to learn to trust him.

THE ASSEMBLAGE

It was a bright, mild winter morning, and the railway station was brimming and brewing with life. Three million people would pass in and out of this old Victorian structure today. It wasn't a special day; 3 million people passed through it every day.[1] A band of boys stood in a corner near the book stall. Their eyes were glued to the south entrance of the railway station. While others were awaiting their trains, these boys were waiting for Mordechai. An old, tired-looking clock hung lifeless from the ceiling close to one of the station exits. Although it seemed dead, it dictated the time. It was 10:00 a.m. when Mordechai arrived.

There was a strange silence. Glances passed between each other, and bodies seemed to fidget with nervousness, but Mordechai stood calmly before them. He had all the time in the world. He would wait for them to answer his greeting. He would wait to win their hearts. Suddenly, six-year-old Achim yelled out loud, "Hello!" His face split into a grin and with a similar suddenness, he lowered his eyes and stared at the dirty floor below him. But with that hello a conversation began almost out of nothing. Mordechai listened to each one intently, his eyes searching, seeking, and studying. He loved these boys. He wanted to take them home and look after them. He wanted to *be* home to them.

It had taken two years to sort it out with the boys, to earn their trust. They were young and tender and much wounded. They had been homeless children in a city where many spend the night on the streets. They were broken inside and had aged way beyond their years, and yet they still had all the innocence of childhood in the tender, trusting look in their eyes, in their nervous smiles and meaningless giggles, in their nudging and fidgeting. It could also be seen in the wild pain of bitter memories that made them roll on the ground shrieking, shaking, and convulsing, a pain that was very tangible, very thick, very dark. When the darkness hit, Mordechai would spring to attend to their pain to provide a healing touch. He was always there watching and ready. Like he had done with Moses, he would

---

[1] UNESCO, Chhatrapati Shivaji Terminus (formerly Victoria Terminus), http://whc.unesco.org/en/list/945

hold them in his arms and rock them back and forth, one with them and their sorrows, merging and forming deeper bonds.

Moses accepted his new brothers with the joy of a whimpering puppy. He had more people to talk to, to play with, to share. It was looking good for Moses. The tide was rough most of the time in the year that followed, but Mordechai went on. He went on loving them and doing things for them, feeding them and providing for them. He relied on the Lord and sought His provision one day at a time. And now it was time to send the kids to school.

One fine morning the band woke up to embrace their first day in school. Their young hearts beat violently. Their hearts had always pounded hard when they saw people their age in school uniforms. They felt insecure, uncertain if they would fit in. But Mordechai had spent a lot of time mentoring them and preparing them for this day. He was excited for them! He knew the importance of education and was thankful that they were able to go to school now.

One of the children that Mordechai had rescued was Barack. He was seven years old. He had been sleeping on the street adjacent to a big, private school until Mordechai had found him and brought him home. Barack had been a child slave before, and he was forced to beg for food and money at the nearby railway station. Each morning as Barack made his way to beg at the railway station, he had watched moms and dads walking hand in hand with their sons and daughters toward the school gate. It made him sad. It was a sad vision that his tender years had not prepared him for. He felt angry and upset, but he could not show it. As a result, it wasn't easy for Barack to go to school with the other children each day. In fact, it wasn't easy for any of them. Going to school each day was like stepping into an unfamiliar world. It seemed like an ocean full of strange creatures. The atmosphere was too cold, and there were rules for everything. You did what the teacher said and followed the rest. You greeted everyone and smiled even when you did not really want to. You even ate at fixed times and not just when you felt hungry. You were made to read, write, and think of nice things and speak and tell others in the classroom about it. It was an ocean where everyone else knew what to do, and the others seemed cleverer and brighter and better all the time. And it all felt very, very uncomfortable.

BARACK'S FIRST DAY AT SCHOOL

Barack went to school; it was his first day.
His head was full of fear, but he dared not say.
Mordechai left him at the school gates;
he saw classrooms and teachers and lots of mates.

He felt homesick; he missed the streets,
he wanted something familiar.
He wished there'd be someone to greet,
a friend perhaps to chatter.

And although those streets had been mean to him,
a school such as this he had hardly seen.
He had worked on the streets since he was four;
he had begged for food and done much more.

But a book full of pictures he had never owned;
a box full of biscuits, a cake, and cone.
And although nice things happened in school,
the first days were like a large whirlpool.

But every now and then they came,
those bitter memories and the pain.
Now he had learned how to cope;
he folded his hands and to God he spoke.

❄ ❄ ❄

*   *   *

And time passed by; now he is a teen.
He wears nice red shirts and dark blue jeans.
He studies real hard and gets good grades;
he helps at home and everyone he aids.

He is getting stronger;
I mean within.
He strives to move on;
he holds high his chin.

One day he plans to visit those streets
where life was bitter and full of deceit.
He wants to find other sad Baracks;
take them to school and give them a snack.

He never forgets to thank the Creator
Who saved him and gave him his laughter.
Had it not been for Mordechai,
Barack would have surely died.

So keep your eyes open; see what you cannot!
There is so much to do; all you need is a thought.
Spare some time each day and just look around,
God is waiting for you, just listen to the sound.

RUTH

The band of boys grew in numbers over the next years, and Mordechai began building his own little nest, along with Ruth. Ruth was a young lady who worked at his old office. She had been working in the administrative department. Mordechai liked her a lot, and he was surprised when he found her at his home one morning.

Ruth had been disappointed when Mordechai left the company where they had worked together for many years. Ruth had thought about him often and decided to find him. She heard about Mordechai's new life, so she decided to meet up with him. She wasn't really prepared for this visit and was surprised to see a bunch of bright, young, happy faces surrounding her all at once. Any new visitor was very welcome in this home, and Ruth was a very beautiful lady. She had a lovely, pearly smile, and her dark eyes smiled all the time too. The children were captivated by her demeanor.

Moses was the first one to introduce himself. Mordechai was not at home when Ruth arrived. As he stepped into the room an hour or so later, he found Ruth seated on the floor surrounded by the boys. They were reading a book together.

A year later, Mordechai married Ruth. Ruth was young and she knew what she wanted. She wanted to be his wife and an integral part of Mordechai's new family. It was a small wedding and a very rare one at that. There were ten best men and no bridesmaids. Ruth was happy having some of the best men she knew by her side.

HOME OF LOVE

Ruth's presence brought about a dramatic change in everyone's life. The house looked nicer. Wildflowers bobbed happily in a glass of water on the table near the window. The kitchen was full of activity. The aroma of freshly cooked food swept through the rooms each day. The linen was fresh and clean. The beds were all made up each morning. Birthdays and special days were celebrated. Everyone had chores assigned to them. Everyone had a place in the family and an identity of his own. There was a need to be, to live.

The kids loved celebrations. It was Father's Day and a very special day for the kids. They prepared skits and plays, sung songs, and played games. Each one wanted to present his skills and talent to Mordechai. They wanted him to see their love, the love that they had learned to receive and give from him over the years. Ruth had ordered chicken biryani from a small family enterprise in the market, where fresh food was cooked as ordered each day. Chicken biryani is an aromatic mix of basmati rice and chicken cooked together with fresh herbs and spices. The children loved it. It was their favorite celebration food, and their faces lit up as Ruth bent over each one's plate and piled it with a large helping.

Mordechai put them to bed that evening, hugging each one, letting them know how much he appreciated them. However, this year, the celebration had aroused a lot of emotions in Mordechai. He was overwhelmed with all the love God had brought into his life through these children. The manner in which God had been relentlessly providing for them and making it possible for him, an ordinary man to live such a fulfilling life, made Mordechai deeply thankful. Since Ruth was exhausted, he insisted on her going to bed early and took on the dishes and cleaning up that night. It was very quiet.

Mordechai heard the sound of a bunch of keys and the closing of a lock outside his door. It was his neighbor leaving for the night shift at the cigarette factory a couple of miles away. And then there was silence again. Mordechai's thoughts drifted to his village in Orissa—his childhood. His father had never acknowledged him as a son. He had had no role model to follow until he got hold of the Bible one day. A Christian missionary had been visiting his school, and the kids were each given a free Bible. Most of them had left it in school and forgotten about it, but Mordechai loved reading; books were difficult to afford and a free book was always welcome. As he read the New Testament, he met a God who he could relate to. Over the years, Mordechai grew in his relationship with God. The Father in heaven had now become his own personal Father too.

God was now teaching him to be a good father to these children; they brought out his potential. Their broken past challenged him. He worked hard to meet their emotional needs and they loved him immensely in return. What do you do when you live in a country, where there are large pockets of people living in shattering poverty? A country where there are never enough homes for the underprivileged, homes that have well-trained counselors and mentors, doctors and caretakers, like you see in the Western world.

We may give up, undone by the sheer magnitude of the situation, but God does not. Through Mordechai, God has shown me what is possible through one ordinary person. We can do all things, if we let Him use us. He has the means, He has the strength, He has the resources, and He rules this planet. He is sovereign. No wonder then that Mordechai never lacks; his resource is God Himself.

It was April and the summer holidays broke in. The kids got through their academic year well enough. There were mixed feelings in the room that evening, just before the beginning of the summer of 2008; after all, it wasn't just a normal summer break for Prashanth and Rohan who had finished their schooling this summer. They were excited and nervous at the same time. Prashanth wanted to be an architect, and Rohan wanted to teach. The younger ones were oblivious to any of this. For them it was a normal summer holiday; a time spent in learning music, playing cricket, and helping out with the house chores. And then there was summer camp! Mordechai took the entire band camping for a week. That was a summer ritual. They went out trekking in the hills and lived outdoors. It was the most exciting part of summer.

A HOME OF LOVE

Let me acquaint you with the clan!
There's Barack, Zakkai, Ehud, and Ethan,
Carmi and Reue, Jonah and Stephen.
They huddle up together; they wear wristbands.
'Tween sports and study, their time is well planned.

Peas in a pod are Nathan and Raphael,
they love disorder; their clothes are a pile!
Neriah like a lamp he shines;
Moses loves fish, he never declines.

Pallu and Shiloh have left the nest;
Prashanth and Rohan are giving it their best.
And yes there's Aron, a high mountain he will be;
together these people make a sweet family.

Ruth and Mordechai have built a sanctum
where love and sharing is a custom.
It's a place where guests are treated as angels;
there is rice and papad and lots of nice pickles.

A home of love this truly is.
God resides here; this home is His!

SUMMER OF 2008

It was a summery, breezy night and Mordechai lay on a bed made of jute ropes, his eyes shut, his thoughts drifting through the corridors of his past. A cool wind was blowing, the stars were gleaming above, and the night was filled with shadows, shadows that kept changing their shapes and sizes, as the moon inched its way through the night sky.

Mordechai watched those shadows meditatively. He felt like they were watching him too—looking out for him rather. He often felt them around, these shadows. And they were the kind that didn't threaten but made him feel safe; perhaps, they were the shadows of the angels God has assigned to watch over him and his family.

As his eyes began to droop, he woke up to a rustle. A little puppy had made his way to the edge of his bed and had been rubbing his back gently on the wooden leg below. He seemed to come out of nowhere. Mordechai rolled it upward gently into his arms and instantly decided to keep it with them, at least as long as the camp lasted. There was a lot of space here, and the boys would love to have him around. He got off the bed and gently placed the puppy in one of the boy's tents. He could anticipate the happy squeals from the tent the next morning.

As he lay back on the bed of jute ropes again, he thought about the dying man whom he had mistaken to be grime many years ago, Moses's father. *There is a rising in death*, he thought, *an awakening. It is never the end of it all.* One tragic death had changed the course of his life here on earth. One man's death had allowed many children the dignity and joy of life. "Mr. Grime" would never know it perhaps, but his death had brought about some good. His death sowed a seed that grew into a huge banyan tree, under which many orphans have found their purpose and live fruitful lives.

CAN ONE HEART
HOUSE SO MANY?

Mordechai's ability to love has often astonished me! I have met many generous souls over the years, and I have also had encounters with wicked ones, but I have been very humbled by Mordechai's heart toward his adopted sons. In his home of love, there are no favorites.

To love each child in a clan and enable him to live fearlessly, believing that he is no less precious than the rest, you need supernatural intervention. You need God to give you His heart. Mordechai loves these precious ones passionately. His love isn't overbearing nor stifling. His love enables them; it sets them free to discover their identity, to recognize and believe that they have a Father in heaven Who loves them. It is a love that neither constrains nor suppresses.

Such love nourishes the soul, and its deeds etch and imprint the words *wanted* and *loved* in your innermost being forever. Your idiosyncrasies are wanted. Your absence is felt. You are unique, unmatched, and unparalleled. A child needs that. We all do.

By April 2013, Moses and most of the old gang had moved on. They are gainfully employed, and they sparkle in this land like jewels in a crown, making a difference through their actions of love. As a child grows up and is gainfully employed, Mordechai helps him to move on and a new child joins the family. There is a new gang now; they are out at school writing their final examinations before the summer break. Mordechai is praying and fussing over each one of them, feeding them, and helping them with their studies just like he did with Moses, Barack, and the rest. But the examinations will be over soon, and it will be time for summer camp once again!

MORDECHAI

Mordechai is a short man; he is all of five feet five inches — an ordinary man who goes unnoticed on the streets. His life has changed mine forever and each encounter with him leaves me overwhelmed; it presents a moment of challenge, a challenge to change, to grow and to give. Mordechai is a manifestation of God's love.

Mordechai's story actually began even before his encounter with Moses's father on the streets of Mumbai. He came to Mumbai for the first time in 1992 on a holiday. He grew up in a small village in Orissa and like most young people his age, Mordechai wanted to visit the commercial capital of India. As he wandered through the streets and alleys of Mumbai and traveled on the trains, he was immensely moved by the street urchins all over. Those harsh pictures of children begging, of them being beaten and roughed up, never left Mordechai. In 1993, he returned to Mumbai to work with a nongovernmental organization (NGO). He quit after a few years and began working full time to better the lives of a handful of street children like Moses, who had no future. During his years at the NGO, he had received apt training in the same areas of work, and that experience helped. Mordechai was able to handle these dramatic situations with a lot of professionalism and care.

He related an encounter with a child in 1992 on his holiday in Mumbai.

As I wandered through the streets and alleys of Mumbai and traveled on the trains, I was immensely moved by the street urchins all over. One afternoon as I stood at a fast-food stall outside a railway station, eating a snack and sipping my chai, a little child came begging. I refused to give him money and instead offered him some food, which the child readily accepted. I was a bit out of sorts with the pace of the city, and as I kept watching people buzz in and out all around me, I suddenly heard the child I had just offered some food to crying out vociferously. He was being beaten with a stick by a local policeman. I could not justify this action in my heart and asked the people around who were intently watching, passive and unperturbed, as to the reason behind this cruelty. All I got as an answer were muffles and embarrassed laughter. The sound of that laughter haunted me. My heart yearned to hold that child and soothe his wounds.

Mordechai heard the Call and answered it. With God as his Provider, he worked and shared all that he had, and set up a home for these children later on. Years went by after that encounter in 1992, but Mordechai could never get those images out of his mind. He was destined to meet Moses. In Moses, Mordechai met God Himself.

But what inspires me and moves me is his role as Daddy and how amazingly well he carries it out. Such a task is not for the weak hearted. It is not about setting up a charity or staying on the periphery and supporting from outside, although all of that is necessary too; but most of us would rather give some money than choose to be Daddy or Mommy to a homeless child. These children need love; they need recognition, a sense of belonging, and it is possible with God's supernatural intervention to provide that to these innocent lives. You need God to give you His heart.

In Mordechai, I see the heart of God, a heart that is large enough to accommodate the sufferings and pain of many lost children—children without parents, living on the streets, broken and abused because of their circumstances. He has built a labyrinth of love and kindness, warmth and generosity, around these children; he has given them their childhood.

My first encounter with Mordechai was very out of the ordinary. His gentleness and simplicity, his calm composure, and his bright smile that could enable a dozen bulbs to shine all at once made him eminently endearing. In Mordechai I met a man who lived his faith out. His relationship with God was his addiction.

His being encapsulates vulnerability and power living in harmony. It's his vulnerability toward God that empowers him to do things that most of us do not do. His vulnerability is his virtue—a virtue that comes to his aid as he walks on his quicksand. He walks on it with dignity, fully knowing that the Power of powers resides in him. He has learned the most valuable lesson of all: how to receive love and how to give it. I salute him!

FOR RUTH AND MORDECHAI

"Where you go I will go, and where you stay I will stay.
Your people will be my people and your God my God.
Where you die I will die, and there I will be buried.
May the Lord deal with me, be it ever so severely,
if even death separates you and me."

Ruth 1:16–17

PART 2: MOONSTONE

MOONSTONE

Dear Moon, so many have written about you,
about your serene beauty in the night sky.
They've romanced you and courted you,
but did they see the reflection of your Creator?

You reflect a mystery that is deep,
filled with peace and power all in one.
Of things eternal that cannot be seen,
of worthy things that yet have to be done . . .

This is Esther's story.
She is my dear friend. Her uncompromising faithfulness
to her Call continues to inspire me each day.
She is my moonstone.

KNOCKS

Esther's walk on the quicksands of human trafficking began one Friday afternoon when she heard the knock. She heard it loud and clear.

Knocks are so anticipative in nature, aren't they? When someone knocks at the door at home, or in your office, all your senses divert and focus on that knock; you could have been waiting for that knock for a long time, or perhaps you were not really expecting one, or wanting one at that moment.

I had working parents and among many other things, in the bosom of my childhood memories, are those anticipative knocks. Each day I would wait for those knocks. They came in the form of a doorbell, or at times it was just a woody, sharp sound on the door. And the knocks were distinct! I had trained my ears to recognize knocks and doorbells. I knew when it was Dad out there or Mom. Those knocks had their individual personality inscribed on them. When Dad knocked at the door, it was always urgent and loud, and when Mom knocked on the door, it was a light, soft sound like that of a ripe coconut hitting the sand floor.

There would be days when I wasn't ready for it though. There would be a knock just at that precise moment, when my hands would be busy digging into a jar of prawn pickles, or I would be in the midst of gobbling up delicious homemade goodies, which were meant to be eaten at certain fixed times only. And then there were days when I just could not wait to hear that knock! There was so much to share with Mom and Dad about my day, or so much to discuss about our evening outing—where we would be going and to which movie or restaurant. My parents always prolonged the surprises as long as they could, and as kids we had a lot of time to imagine and anticipate.

But when the Supernatural steps into your natural world—when God knocks on your door—what do you do? How do you recognize it? Do you even want to? God came knocking on Esther's door that afternoon as we were sipping our coffee together. Esther anticipated that if she opened the door, her world, her life, would certainly change for an eternity.

RESTLESS WHISPERING

It was a cold and dry January morning in Vienna. The year 2005 had ushered itself in a fortnight ago. I strode up the steep stairs that led to Pastor Anath's office. It was a small, warm room with lots of books. A lady stood at the edge of the table. She seemed to be frowning at something she was still reading on the laptop. And then all at once her attention was diverted; she looked up at me. Her eyes were soft and tender, her gaze deep. They were searching, seeking, warm and friendly, all at the same time.

It had been two years since I moved to Vienna, and she would become a very dear friend in this Ville de la Musique. My first impression of Esther was that of a compassionate person. I felt I would have a friend in Vienna at last! We have shared and experienced much together since that first wintry day in January. I want you to meet her too. Let's journey together through her quicksand. In 2007, Esther was forty-four years old, a mother of three adults, and the last one had just left home. Esther and her husband, Anath, were coping with an empty nest.

Esther was sitting in on a seminar conducted by a group of women from mixed backgrounds in Europe. The seminar took place in Vienna, and the subject was human trafficking. She had invited me to the seminar. What we heard at that seminar was devastating and heartbreaking. The evils of human trafficking, the snares, and the networks in Europe, it disturbed me. I grew up in the city of Mumbai in India. I had not been really exposed to the world of street women there. It had evaded me because of my overprotected childhood and my career choices; they formed geographical boundaries that I never crossed. I grew up knowing and hearing of such things but never really having to confront it. But there were no such geographical boundaries to protect me now. Vienna was a relatively smaller city of 1.7 million people, and it was not uncommon, until 2007, to see women propositioning on the streets, sometimes even during the day.

During our break from the seminar, we both looked contemplative and stared deeply into our mugs of coffee in the cafeteria, as if they were bottomless pits beckoning to be jumped into. Esther remembered a conversation we had had not so long ago in the warmth of her sitting room. We had been talking about moving out of our comfort zones. She bobbed up her head as if an electric current had shot its way up through her spinal cord; she looked at me sighing deeply with watery eyes and a half-broken smile. "Jen, I think I need to get out of my comfort zone now," she softly whispered.

Esther and Anath left their home in the United States and arrived in Vienna in 1989. In their early days in Vienna, Esther lived in an apartment that brought her into uncomfortable closeness at times with the ugly world of human trafficking. She had watched the street below her window in restless contemplation. The women, all painted and dressed, were propositioning on the streets, and her heart had cried out, *This cannot be. This is not how it is meant to be! That beautiful young girl, she must be barely seventeen. She should be in high school right now having fun with people her age. This is not meant to be!*

Those silent frustrations and restless whisperings never left Esther. They came rapidly over the years in different forms, and each time her heart had cried out, *This is not how it is meant to be!*

FOR YOU BRAVE HEARTS!

"You are my hiding place;
You will protect me from trouble and surround me
with songs of deliverance."

Psalm 32:7

It hurts when I see you; I bleed inside.
I want you to know, I'm on your side.
You've been ravaged and torn apart in two,
but, Lady, today I bow to you!

You've taught me to redefine brokenness and pain,
my journey and yours are not the same.
You've been beaten and bruised, torn and jilted;
the marks you bear, they leave you daunted.

I go to bed on a fluffy pillow each night;
that's when your day begins, and all your plight.
And you still dare to smile, it's not the flashy grin;
a smile that can be read, if seen from within.

But alas such smiles, folks can't interpret,
for their hearts are dark and full of covet.
They say you chose this way of life,
their words dig deep, they can't see your strife.

Your heart has hardened; you are scared to even breathe,
for no one hears you, even when you plead.
And there's a girl hidden, a soul that's bidden
to strip, to bare, to be scarred beyond repair.

He, too, was bruised and broken like you,
but He did it for me, He did it for you.
He cries with you; He was stripped, too.
He knows you, dear lady. He has a name for you.

And you're going to heal, much as it seems surreal.
Look, He has risen. He lives and is able.
He is able to do what you cannot;
He will do it for you, just wire Him a thought.

He has made you His bride, the apple of His eye.
He will tear them to bits, Him they can't defy!
And I know these words, they seem hollow to you,
but I hope it will cheer you, for a moment or two.

So if you want to dare to scale that great wall,
just go, do it, no matter if you fall!
For your freedom has been bought, the price has been paid;
He finished the job, the rules have been laid.

You are a winner through and through,
a crown of jewels is awaiting you.
But you need to step out, you need to break loose.
Claim that freedom, it matters what you choose.

A fallen angel in the dust is not your destiny,
you were made to rule, a princess to be.
Cinderella managed to get her due,
but that was a fairy tale; your story is true!

You don't need a slipper or a magic spell,
just call on His name; the fears will dispel.
A healed soul, a new body,
a sinless world and a new story.

Let's go; eternity is calling!
Spaceships and stars are all rocking.
The lights are bright, there is music, too;
the saxophone for me and the piano for you.

He will wipe all our tears and take away the pain.
We will sigh with happiness; we will breathe again!

CIEL CALLING

Ciel knocked on Esther's door, and she opened it. She stood bewildered with what she saw and with all that transpired in the next couple of minutes.

A Man stood at that door. He wasn't Prince Charming, and He didn't carry roses to greet Esther. He looked outraged. He was livid. His dark chestnut hair hung wild around His shoulders. He looked like he had been in the midst of a battle. His eyes were full of wrath, flaming with passion, almost turbulent. He carried bruises all over Himself. His smooth, bare chest was blemished with scars, like the kind left behind by razor-edged swords and daggers; some scars were old and some looked raw and fresh. He was breathing heavily, and even as He stood there all wounded, His presence was powerful, dominating in sweet ways. The air smelled of a mix of lily-of-the valley and sweet alyssum. He wasn't smiling, but as His eyes met Esther's, they were dancing all of a sudden. Dancing with delight saying hello, the kind of hello that is usually accompanied with crushing hugs and squeals, that say so many things simultaneously.

He stretched out His arm to her. It was a long, strong golden-brown arm. There were currents of urgency radiating, pulsing, imploring almost, from that outstretched arm, and Esther felt it. It had a captivating pull, and yet Esther knew that she would have to clench that arm of her own free will; He would not force her. Esther's heart was throbbing at a deafening pitch; she could not decipher her thoughts. She wanted to clutch at that open arm for life itself, but a huge cloud of doubt seemed to overshadow her desire, estranging her with darkness of a kind that was so thick that you could feel it; it overwhelmed her senses.

She looked up into His blazing eyes, almost pleading Him to understand her dilemma. He gazed down at her adoringly. His gaze sent radiant streams of love and passion searing through her skin and permeating through her entire being, her soul. Esther lowered her eyelids almost instantly, like you do when you can't bear the intensity of pure, bright light. But this light did not hurt her eyes; the intensity of it just kept penetrating and piercing her heart. She dared look into His eyes once again, feeling like she couldn't resist it anymore; the pull was so engaging and winning.

As their eyes met yet again, Esther saw movement, flashes, colors, and people. The outstretched arm held her willing hand and led her onto a battlefield. She found herself in the middle of what can be best described as a world at war and at peace, all at once!

Esther found herself walking in the midst of war lions and celestial beings on one side; on the other side were evil spirits, gruesome beasts, and enormous dragons with red horns that lashed out their tongues spewing out fire clouds at the war lions. The war lions were ferocious and fascinating. They were much larger than the one's we have on our planet. These war lions were magnificent. Their thick mane was a color hard to describe; it was a mix of fiery orange streaks and a deep midnight blue, and their honey-colored skin seemed velvety, soft, gleaming like molten honey. They were ferocious and yet beautiful.

It wasn't a typical battlefield like you see in the movies. It was happening in a prodigious garden of sorts. There were gigantic angels and handsome warriors all clad in white. They moved with a purpose, fully convinced of their mission. However, they seemed strangely joyous, in the midst of a battlefield! There were victory cries in the form of melodious music, booming from varied corners of this seemingly boundaryless garden battlefield. The mighty warriors already knew how the battle would end, and yet so much depended on their conviction, on their skills, and on their commitment at that particular moment. There was no time to be distracted. Eternity itself seemed to be at stake. Alongside, she heard deep moans and grunts. Haunting lament echoed through barren spaces.

As these spaces came into sight, she could see the ground around all charred and lifeless. Huge infernos erupted, ejecting ash and brimstone at a distance, and somewhere else closer to the victory cries, thick, black smoke magically turned into silvery, golden smoky wafers meandering with the wind.

The condors and kites swooped down and supplied the joyous forces with ammunition, feeding them with energizing nutriment. This nutriment looked like crispy, creamy wafers, which seemed to provoke the white-clad warriors into even more zestful, vigorous battle.

The war lions and the celestial beings fought alongside the gigantic angels and the handsome warriors. They fought against the gruesome beasts, the dragons, and the evil spirits. These evil spirits looked terrifying, menacing, and too horrendous to describe. They were of the kind that made you feel creepy, sick, and terrified immediately. They were huge, their eyes were a deep red, and their skin seemed similar to that of crocodiles — flaky, thick, and full of sludge. They all looked menacing and loathsome.

But the joyous army seemed to be slaughtering them with ease, and as the evil beasts fell to the ground thousands at a time, the garden battlefield metamorphosed into Eden. An endlessly sprawling garden of colors, abounding with life where murmuring birds seamlessly glided in and out. The melodies rocked one's heart with multifarious emotions of an ethereal kind, unknown and yet familiar. Rivers burst forth from the mountains in the backdrop, and silver diamond streams of water rippled through woods. Somewhere there was thunder and lightning, and elsewhere a gigantic rainbow was on display in colors one had never seen before. Tulips, roses, lilies, and daffodils — all the size of melons — seemed to be burgeoning out of the earth. The dry, cracked ground was turning into a rich, green carpet. And the transformation was happening rather quickly; the pace seemed to have intensified.

Esther saw herself on that battlefield in Ciel. She was putting on her armor, a white armor like all of the rest, with blazing red inscriptions on it that read: *The army of the Lion of Judah*. A magnificent golden war lion was waiting to take her onto the battlefield. She needed no further convincing. She joined the battle of the joyous, the army of the Lion of Judah.

THE SQUAD

It was five in the morning, and spring was settling in. The barn swallows and the black birds were in melodious company, along with other birds that had come back home in the spring. Esther woke up remembering her encounter with the tall, dark Man Who had carried a hurricane in His chest. He had taken her into the battlefield in Ciel itself. She had witnessed the ongoing battles for Eden. It wasn't just one battle. There were several battles that were being fought simultaneously. The art of warfare was as varied as the battles themselves were. Some battles were being fought with weapons of love and understanding, patience, kindness, and giving, while other battles were ferocious and a lot of blood was being shed.

It had been a dream, but Esther knew it to be real, as real as her very existence here on earth. She had joined the legion of the Night Riders under the banner of the Lion of Judah. They were engaged in the battle to liberate slaves, to break bondages, to cover naked, mutilated bodies, and to love the unloved. This was a dream that had earthly consequences. As she stood by her coffee roaster waiting for a freshly brewed cup of coffee, she mulled over the Psalm she had read last night.

Who is like the Lord our God,
The One who sits enthroned on high,
Who stoops down to look on the heavens and the earth?
He raises the poor from the dust and lifts the needy from the ash heap;
He seats them with princes, with the princes of His people.

Psalm 113:5–8

Much happened over the next two years. Esther faced many impediments. Her motives were questioned. But each trial brought with it a certainty, a conviction. What lay before her wasn't easy. It wasn't easy to articulate her conviction to work and serve women in prostitution. From repulsion, pessimism, and acceptance, Esther's world reacted in different ways.

Esther moved on and forged ahead with those who accepted her vision and believed in her cause. Many hearts were moved when they heard Esther speak, when she made her case against human slavery in Vienna. Now was the time to do, to act. Eventually, around twenty people, mostly women, joined Esther with a common purpose. Their mission was to share the unconditional love of God with women who worked in the field of prostitution.

Esther remembers their first Christmas outreach. The atmosphere was fevered with passion and purpose. Esther and her squad visited fifteen bars and a large complex that had apartments built and intended for prostitution. They distributed cakes, coffee, homemade cookies, and beautifully wrapped gifts to hundreds of women. Over that Christmas season, they reached out to four hundred women, women who suffered greatly at that time. They suffered from childhood memories of Christmas; they suffered from being separated from their loved ones; they suffered from cold and loneliness.

The squad went out week after week after that, seeking conversations with these women. These vulnerable, beautiful women stood on street corners late at night decked out in makeup and very little clothing, signaling, hoping, hating. I have often heard people refer to them as "those women." Those women who lure and seduce men. Those women who entice the men to come and spend a few minutes, a few hours, or an entire night with them huddled up among the bushes, behind the bus stop, or in a posh five-star hotel room. It depended on the client's affluence and the mood he was in. He was paying the bills, after all.

They sell their bodies. They do not sell themselves. Let me share with you what I have learned from Esther about these brave hearts.

STREET CONVERSATIONS

Esther and her friends were delighted that their Christmas street project had turned into a regular activity. The encounters and conversations were real. Friday evenings were street evenings. The squad set out across different parts of the city every Friday evening to meet their new acquaintances, to build friendships, to serve, and to help these beautiful yet badly broken women of the night. The encounters and conversations infused the squad with feelings of deep sadness and frustration. But through these dark conversations, they got to meet the *real* jewels. They found spirits that were strong, brave, optimistic, still hopeful, and still believing. Each visit from the squad was a visit from Hope itself. These warm and friendly encounters mellowed down the lines of horror and tragedy from their faces for a few moments; it allowed these women to experience lighthearted laughter and joy for a while.

Esther remembered her first meeting with one of these brave hearts, which she would never forget. She was standing on the street at a popular traffic signal in the city. It was late evening, and as the signal lights changed to red, she saw Angelia sashaying her way toward an open Volkswagen window. Esther could not see much because it was a cold, dark, and somewhat foggy evening, but just as Esther began turning her head away, a huge truck sped up in the opposite direction and beamed its headlights directly on Angelia. Esther had a good look at her profile. She hesitated for a few seconds; she wanted to talk to this young girl, but Angelia was too busy at that Volkswagen window. Esther crossed the street and moved on with Angelia's profile etched on her heart. Angelia's confident posture as she propositioned on the street had not convinced Esther. Esther felt a stirring in her heart. She could not squelch those stirrings, and they lingered.

Angelia's profile kept haunting Esther. Each Friday evening, Esther looked out for Angelia; she could not forget that profile. She got to know a few women during those first evenings, and some felt comfortable enough to meet Esther for lunch in the city, but Angelia didn't turn up until summer. It was another late, very hot Friday evening. Temperatures in Vienna had risen abnormally over the week and had touched 38°C (100.4°F). The sun had just set, and the air was thick with humidity. Esther pulled out her bottle of water and just as she leaned her head backward to take a swig, she saw that profile again, the one she had been yearning to see all these months!

Esther had been waiting at her usual Friday evening spot. She had just stepped out of the van a couple of minutes ago and was hoping to meet up with a seventeen-year-old girl whom she had run into the week before. She was a young Romanian who had fled from the clutches of an atrocious mother. She had been sold off to a brothel in the town of Timisoara. Angelia saw Esther too. She had seen Esther and the squad who came out on Friday evenings to her district and talked to her colleagues before. She watched Esther slowly walk up to her; it made her feel skittish and out of sorts. She never really liked talking with anyone. Esther went up to Angelia and asked her if she would have the time to walk down the alley with her to a small café and have a thirst quencher together. Angelia refused at first; it was high business time and she had bills to pay, but despite herself, she nodded with a shy smile in agreement, and they made their way to the café.

ANGELIA

Angelia was once a little girl, just like you and me;
she loved to dance and twirl, and play with beetle bees.

She grew up before her time had come; her heart was still so tender.
From the big, bad world she tried to run, but the evil witch got hold of her.

The witch promised her a cruise and cast a spell on Angelia.
She bought her dresses and shoes and taught her to cha-cha.

She took her to a big, dark city, and there sold her to a beast.
He hurt her and showed no mercy; he made her work, so he could feast.

She is standing in the cold; it is freezing outside.
The snowflakes are falling; the night's a long ride.

She shuffles and wails, Angelia is lamenting.
But to no avail, her client is waiting.

She disappears into the snowstorm; she dies inside some more.
Pain awaits her in the morn; he'll handle her like a boar.

She seeks to run out of town; who can she trust?
They have all let her down and trampled her to dust.

She is one of those sand grains; please lift one up,
hold it under a lens and see the close-up!

Every grain is a jewel in the waiting; go bring out her real beauty.
Adorn her with love and caring; she is soul more than body.

You and me, we can save Angelia; she needs protection and esteem.
Let's take this sand grain to the Delta; she'll shimmer like a galaxy in stream.

There are many sand grains out there, trodden on and treated with contempt.
Don't wait too long, just simply care; it's worth more than all you've dreamt.

YOU MUST KNOW

In these quicksands of drudgery, rape and assault, greed and humiliation, there is such emptiness and pain; it must break us too. How can it not?

Brie was five years old when she was raped, and she didn't even know it. She was raped by her stepfather; he kidnapped her later on and locked her in a wooden cabin deep in the middle of a forest in winter. Her stepfather would visit her each evening, give her a bit of food, rape her, and lock her in the small, dark cabin again. The cabin had no electricity and no windows. It was damp and cold, and Brie lived there for six months. When she was broken beyond rebellion, she was taken to a faraway land and sold off to a brothel.

Sammy was sold by her own mother at the age of sixteen to a pimp. She had not known, until then, that her mom was a prostitute.

Misaki looked like a beautiful blossom, which is what her name really means. Now, she is thirty years old and has four children. She still looks like a blossom, bruised and crushed most of the time though. Her husband makes an appearance every now and then, takes her money, rapes her, and whips her—in that order—every single time.

Rosalia and Kayin are close. They have been on the streets since they were sixteen, and now it's been eight long years. Kayin is such a beautiful name; it means "celebrated." She was the only child. Her parents sent her to school one day, and she was kidnapped by a lady who turned out to be a whore. She was made to travel on a dilapidated ship across countries with other illegal migrants. Through storms and sands, she sailed and walked for months on end with hardly anything to eat. She was gang raped on the ships, beaten, stripped in the midst of men, and made to do things that are perverse. Kayin was a celebrated child. Last year, she had chances to escape, but she doesn't want to go back home. She is full of shame and guilt, and she knows that she will not be accepted.

Anaya is seven months pregnant, and she is still selling her body on the street. The other day she was at the street corner at 4:00 p.m. Four hours later, as the next batch of women came along to begin their soliciting, Anaya was still waiting for her first customer. It's not easy to get a customer when you are pregnant. Anaya was about to head back to her dingy little room in one of the alleys of Vienna when a car pulled up and she got in.

Anushka is twenty years old. She celebrated her birthday at a lovely café with Sarah who works with the squad. Anushka narrated the traumatic experience at the doctor's office when the infected residue of her abortion had been cleaned up. Anushka continues to endanger her life every single day by employing her body to do things it is not capable of.

Jia and Juan were waiting for customers at 9:00 p.m. near the parking lot behind a park. A car stopped in front of them and the men inside claimed to be cops. They flashed false police badges and commanded Jia and Juan to get inside the car. Jia means "beautiful" and Juan stands for "gracious." What happened to these two women in the car in the next hours cannot be described. It was a far cry from their names. They were left scarred and thrown out of the running car in the middle of nowhere. Yes, they are alive. A passerby called the emergency service, and Jia and Juan were taken to a nearby hospital where their wounds were treated with further contempt by several nurses. These nurses seemed to have forgotten that their duty was not to judge but to heal and help, bandage and salvage.

Many of you would have liked me to spare you these details. We have learned to isolate ourselves from it all. Even from the pain of knowing. But you must know. You must know that young Sylvia is suffering from HIV, and her madam wants her to be on the streets every single night. The financial target has to be met or there will be repercussions.

Aisha is twenty-two years old; she spent seven months in a Libyan prison while on her way to Europe through land and sea. There were 190 women with her, and they had just one toilet to share. They were constantly harassed by the prison guards, and some of them took refuge. They sought refuge in God. They lifted up their hands in prayer to the Creator of the universe, and He answered. Aisha was not raped, and she managed to escape. Aisha made it safely to her land of promise. But she knew that her perils were not behind her, and the worst was yet to come. And it came. Aisha was sold to a brothel in one of Vienna's dingiest areas, and she took her God along with her.

Through years of desolation, pain, humiliation, tyranny, and unimaginable ordeals, she has held her hands up in prayer. She hasn't stopped loving her God. She believes that He will come and rescue her. Yes, you may argue and not understand Aisha. But she believes in Him. He has kept her soul free, free to believe in Him, free to praise Him, and to talk to Him. Hope is a priceless gift, especially when you live the life that Aisha is forced to live.

Kareena's father left them when she was ten years old. Kareena's mother is an alcoholic. Kareena wants to buy herself a home and a car. She wants a better life. She knows only one way to it for now and that is by prostituting herself. She says she has no friend in this city. She says, "It is only God and me." Her God waits for her on a special shelf with sliding doors in her cupboard. There is a candle in there, which Kareena lights when she is talking to her God. There are pictures of better times and loved ones. There are trinkets and little gifts that Kareena received as a little girl. This is her hiding place, her sanctuary. She slides open the glass to this shelf when she is alone in her room, when there are no customers whose lustful demands need tending to.

KAREENA'S GOD

Who is this God Who lives in a box?
He sits and waits until you unlock.
You hear Him even when the pain strikes;
the whip is on His back, it's also with spikes.

You go to Him with a mutilated body;
someone's ravaged you and shredded you.
You go to Him with a mutilated soul;
someone's cursed you and burnt you.
They have torn your virtue, but He can undo.

Who is this God Whom you so revere?
Who is He, for He helps you endure.
A holy place for Him you have made
in the middle of your pain,
where you lie down full of shame.

He gives you the strength to talk to Him;
He covers you with white sheets of satin.
He nurses your wounds; He gives you respite
from strangers and neighbors, from friendly traitors.

Is He the same One Who created the heavens and the earth,
the oceans and the mountains, and all our places of birth?
Is He the One Who knit you together?
Your destiny He wrote, He became your Anchor.

Is He the One the Bible talks about?
Jesus of Galilee Who bailed women out?
His encounters with women are worth a read,
our hearts must change; women need to be freed.

WOULD YOU DARE?

We are the wives of nightfall. And yet to learn of kind-
ness after so much unkindness, to understand that a little
girl with more courage than she knew would find that her
prayers were answered; can that not be called happiness?

Film: *Memoirs of a Geisha*

You have probably heard many such sanguinary stories or perhaps this is your first exposure to human trafficking. As I kept hearing these tragic stories, I wondered if I would be willing to meet one of these women, one of these wounded brave hearts. I wonder if you would dare reach out to one such brave heart yourself. Would you sip a cup of coffee with her and lend her a couple of hours of your life? Would you dare walk through the tunnel of her dark world and yet for a few moments show her some light? Would you be the one to traverse through her cave of horrors?

If just for once in your life, would you help break her face into a smile? Would you dare clean her wounds and embrace this beauty shrouded in filth and disdain? Would you reject your feelings of disgust if you find her living right next to you and shopping in your supermarket? If just for once in your life, would you see yourself in her, your daughter, your niece, your sister, your mother, your aunt, your friend? Would you please dare?

DARE IT!

Do you know your womankind
beyond what you see and feel?
The things she bears are out of mind,
a relentless flow of aches and ordeals.

Will you touch the ocean of vulnerability
that roars in your deepest being?
Lady, please would you not flee
as you rummage through the aching?

One says, "Yes, I've been spared the sword;
I live a busy life, time I can't afford.
I feel sorry for these women, I admit it's tragic,
but life goes on and I'm just a cynic."

Another says, "I have had my share,
I wasn't raped, but life's been a nightmare.
Five kids to feed and a fiend for a man;
he sits at home and boozes his time."

The elegant lady is signing a check,
someone's taking her picture for the local press.
Generous with her money, perfect at love,
work and family, and God above.

Many it would shake, if she raised her voice;
a difference she could make with all her poise.
So let's take the chance, let's make a new friend!
Get out of comfort zones, others' fences let's mend!

A woman from the shadows,
let's be the answer to her prayers.
A smile, a hug, a hot coffee mug,
some respite from her nightmares.

I don't dare you to give what discomforts.
I beckon you to love and feel her hurt!

A GLORIOUS NEW START

Listen, a noise on the mountains, like that of a great multitude!
Listen, an uproar among the kingdoms, like nations massing together!
The Lord Almighty is mustering an army for war.
They come from faraway lands, from the ends of the heavens —
The Lord and the weapons of His wrath —

Isaiah 13:4–5

Esther joined the battle against prostitution with her squad in the spring of 2008. They have met hundreds of hurting women who have migrated from Nigeria and east European countries to this rich city. Some of them work in the cruel industry of prostitution to be able to send money to their children back home, children who grow up under the raw sun without a mom or dad to shadow their lives. The squad may not have revolutionized society in Vienna, but they have done something much bigger. They have brought the stories of these bruised women of the streets into our homes by raising the issue of forced and undesired prostitution, by confronting truth, by fighting for justice, by reminding you and me that our God is a God of justice, and we cannot be passive and neutral to something so absolutely despicable. They have created a furrow in many a heart like mine. Esther and her team are a living example of how God can and will use our ordinary existence for His work, to do extraordinary things that have a deeper impact than anything else that we may try to do, out of sheer human effort. God has all the resources; He needs a willing spirit and a thankful heart.

They have planted the unconditional love of God in hundreds of these brave hearts and rescued a few of them from human slavery. Each life is precious. It is not about the numbers; it is about the names, the faces, the families, and the stories. It is about being a candle in the darkness. And their work doesn't simply end by rescuing these beloved women; these precious women are being nursed, loved, cared for, given a home, a job, and are constantly under the vigil of the squad. The ones they have helped rescue from the clutches of prostitution are still under their care and counseling. These free women are now integrating themselves into society and living a life full of hope. The squad has lit up the lives of hundreds of women working in the brothels of Vienna by meeting them and getting involved in their lives and their problems. The situations are as messy as they can get; you need God's heart to be able to hold yourself together and be strong for such women. Just like with Mordechai, God has to give you His own heart to enable you to bear their pain, and yet come up with rational solutions to some very real problems.

These precious women of the night are not allowed to work on most of the streets in Vienna now. But the brothels are open for business as usual. The squad conducts hundreds of outreaches; they were first conducted on the streets too, but it is mainly indoors now. They meet the women in the brothels if they are allowed, and they also meet with them one on one in a café or over a meal, sometimes in their apartments where they live. It all depends on the willingness of the women to open up. Some brothel owners themselves have become receptive to these visits and do not view the squad as folk to be feared.

Relationships are being fostered and built, and Esther's team, which mainly consists of women, has become "aunts" and "grandmothers" to the babies of these brave hearts. Many of these women do not have the potential to escape right now, but most of them want to. The wounds these precious ones have endured won't heal for a very long time, but the pain that flows out of these wounds can be molded into powerful euphonies that touch and inspire the lives of others. These rescued women are the torchbearers for others who are still in chains. The love and compassion they receive will compel them to live, to reach out, to try, to cry, to hope, to smile, to love, and to give again. That is a glorious new start and a merited end to a horrid story.

Is it not amazing, what a handful of ordinary people like you and me can do when we get together with a common purpose, a common calling? Most of the women and men working with Esther have families of their own and many work in regular jobs. However, they find it in themselves to be flexible, not just to make time but to make space in their hearts to hold the burden of others, to cry, and to feel the pain of these unfortunate victims of modern society. They mentor them and counsel them and treat them as individuals made in God's own image, for that is what they are!

Over these seven years since Esther began a home for the heartbroken women of the night, God has opened up doors for her at political and social levels across countries in the EU and the US, and many new initiatives are being taken each day. Her vision has drawn many others to join the legion of the Night Riders under the banner of the Lion of Judah, God Himself! I am thankful for the privilege I have, of watching God's plan for the women forced into prostitution unfold each day, through Esther and her team.

Her work has impacted many ordinary citizens in Vienna; they come forward regularly offering their time, talents, and resources to raise funds that enable the squad to do what it does, and in doing so, their lives change too. When the head of the family begins thinking differently about the women on the streets who work in prostitution, he begins a revolution in his home, and his children grow up remembering that these brave hearts are not to be shunned. They are normal people like you and me, and they deserve to be respected and accepted for their worth as human beings.

Esther and her squad are creating ripples wherever they serve, and these ripples are slowly turning into huge refreshing waterfalls of love and mercy, serving the lonely and broken, with God as its source.

I salute Esther and her squad!

PART 3: BLUE TOPAZ

BLUE TOPAZ

Blue is the sky; it's the Creator's abode.
Blue is the sea, where dolphins whistle and float.
Blue is the planet we call our home.
Blue is all the space and the in-between tones.

Blue is peace; blue is serene.
But there is passion and ice, a sparkling sheen.
She walks on the planet and does her thing,
shields herself with blue, but there is fire within.

Fire to build the broken, fire to sing His song,
fire of the heavenly Father that keeps her strong.
Blue flames are hot, and yet solid as ice,
a touch that heals and burns you inside.

She speaks to your heart; you hear the Creator.
A dovish rhythm, a gurgling river.
Love and mirth, the joy of rebirth,
the smell of fresh rain, upon dry earth.

He whistles that haunting tune
you have heard in the womb.
It's the melody of love and priceless sacrifice.
So precious we are; He paid a dear price.

Listen . . . it's crystal clear blue, tranquil, and true, sung just for you.

Martha has been the reflection of green pastures and quiet waters on days when I have found my feet stuck in quicksands of my own making. She points her finger to the azure blue sky when my head is hung low. She reminds me that I am the daughter of a heavenly Father! She is my blue topaz.

CHILDHOOD

My encounters with Martha opened up unhealed wounds that were heaped up over four decades of my life, wounds that were consigned to the deep hidden spaces of my heart six feet under. I had gotten used to lugging these wounds along for so long that I didn't notice their existence, until a fresh wound came along and opened up the old ones as well.

I learned to hide my true self even as a little girl. A perusal through one of my childhood albums revealed how well I had learned to hide. The pictures depict me as any other happy child, gleeful, anticipative, and bright eyed. But I know that in some of those pictures, I did not really feel that way. I had learned by then that a few nice poses for the camera kept everyone at bay. My childhood memories are captured in pictures and drawings, writings, and poetry; they have been narrated in anecdotes recounted over the years to friends and family, to little children and fellow travelers, but a lot of it was yet sealed within me.

I did my best to pose for the photos, and there were times, of course, when the art of pretension failed to rescue me and I did not succeed. Those were embarrassing moments for all of us present in the studio. My mother took my sister and me to the local photo studio once a year. It was her way of bolting and sealing our childhood memories together with her, but it was an ordeal for me. The intense gaze of the photographer, coupled with his instructions to stand or lean in a certain way, challenged me and brought out the worst in me. I often cast disdainful looks at the photographer, making my displeasure felt. But relent I must, what with Mother standing menacingly right behind me, too close for comfort. On most occasions, however, I did my best to keep all happy. I posed and smiled and no one knew how I truly felt. Those hours in the studio each year made me feel things that were challenging to articulate; my vocabulary and experiences had not evolved enough. I am older now, and I know how those photo sessions made me feel. I felt weak, vulnerable, and exposed.

A BLUE WORLD

Martha too had her share of childhood wounds. She had a hard childhood, and had learned far too early for her age how to deal with rejection and pain. It has been a long time since that childhood though. Martha has evolved into a charming woman; her face radiates her love for life. Martha's motto is to receive each day as a gift from God, to live each day to the fullest, and leave the morrow to Him. Martha is a woman who chose to seek, to delve into her pains until she found the wounded heart of God Himself. She met a God Who held her as she swam through the memories of sufferings and injustices that she had been through as a young teenager. A God Who wanted her and had created her with the very qualities that people did not recognize as gifts to be cherished. They instead took advantage of her qualities and made her seek self-destruction. Martha met a God Who understood because He had suffered too. He has been the wind under Martha's wings ever since!

He grew up before him like a tender shoot,
and like a root out of dry ground.
He had no beauty or majesty to attract us to him,
nothing in his appearance that we should desire him.
He was despised and rejected by mankind,
a man of suffering, and familiar with pain.
Like one from whom people hide their faces
he was despised, and we held him in low esteem.
Surely he took up our pain
and bore our suffering,
yet we considered him punished by God,
stricken by him, and afflicted.
But he was pierced for our transgressions,
he was crushed for our iniquities;
the punishment that brought us peace was on him
and by his wounds we are healed.

Isaiah 53:2–5

HOW MAY I HELP YOU?

At fifty-four, Martha was a mother of four grown-up sons and wife to a very gentle and endearing Josef. I met Martha in the spring of 2011. It was a lovely spring day in May. It's the time when the first rays of sunshine in the morning feel mild and tingly warm on your skin, whispering the advent of summer not so far away. And until such time, spring keeps you busy with its vast display of colors painted on nature's bed of roses, tulips, coltsfoot, white butterbur, and wild yellow celandine bushes bursting forth with life, transforming the sleepy brown floor of the winter forest into a green mossy bed. This new life makes an appeal to all things living and breathing in the woods to wake up and drench themselves in the colors of spring.

As my bus arrived, I felt a kind of sadness grip my heart. In an hour, I would be boarding a train to a destination I had never been to before. I had no means to prepare myself for this encounter, for I did not know the exact purpose behind my visit.

It had been a little over eight years since I moved to the beautiful city of Vienna, and it had grown on me with time. I migrated and crossed continents at the age of thirty-five, and the transition had cost me dearly. My wholehearted attempts to integrate, learn a new language, make new friends, and settle down into a new marriage had unsettled me in many ways. It had drained me of the very essence of my personality and had taken away those precious nuances that made me, me. I felt like I had lost myself in my arduous attempt to blend and fit into this new culture.

I woke up one morning and found myself grounded. I sensed that I could not go through the routine of another day all over again. I had to just stop. I knew I had to reach out for help, and that is precisely what I was doing. I was reaching out for help. I was traveling by train from Vienna to Salzburg to meet Martha. It was a three-hour journey and a quiet and scenic one at that. I had a window seat. As I sipped my coffee, I felt my breath steam up the window. Wiping off the steam, I looked at the large farm houses stacked up on tiny hills surrounded by grasslands dressed with primroses, cowslips, alyssums, and a sprinkle of tiny irises. Large mattresses of lilac-colored periwinkles sprang up from the forest floor. It was exotic and colorful outside my window, but I felt heavy, forlorn, and very, very gray inside.

It took me a while to find my way from the railway station to the tiny chapel where I was to meet Martha. She stood in the doorway looking out for me. My heart thudded away. This was not going to be easy. Martha was a counselor, and I had never been to one before. She was around five feet six and wore a navy blue pullover and light blue jeans. Her thick, curly hair had bright, blondish highlights. Her right hand was set in a cast. Thick glasses hid her blue eyes, making it difficult for me to gauge her feelings. Suddenly, she broke into a friendly grin. A flash of white in my predominantly gray world!

She gave me a small hug that in some way did comfort, momentarily. I was ushered into a big, white room with high ceilings and French windows lining an entire wall. The room was minimally furnished and had a tiny open kitchenette. I noticed a white table with two chairs on either side near the window. As I mechanically moved toward the table, I saw an open diary and an iPhone next to it, clearly indicating the chair had already been reserved. So I took the one opposite. The air in the room made me feel very cold and wooden, or it may have been the sheer anticipation of what was to happen in the next two hours. There was a writing pad on the desk and a tin that contained some kind of a premixed coffee concoction. Martha offered me a cup of the coffee concoction, which I most readily took. It didn't taste like coffee, but it helped keep my hands busy. Holding the hot cup between my fingers, I boldly looked up at Martha, expressing my readiness to move on.

"So what brings you here, Lady? How may I help you?" she asked gently, but I sensed a firm tone in the question. I knew in that moment that this encounter would leave me raw, open, and wounded. Bending my head, I whispered, "I don't know. I don't know why I am here."

We wrestled with the problem for the next two hours. We had one mission, a common goal, and that was to find out what was wrong with me. Martha asked me to start at the beginning. The question overthrew me; how could I chronologically sort out everything that had happened to me ever since I could remember and lay it all down for her like a well-made casserole in such a short time? The task seemed beyond my means. Martha read my mind, or it may have been sheer routine for her. She reframed her question and said, "Jennifer, talk me through your life, ever since you came to Vienna eight years ago." I sat there struggling to distill and sift through the reams of information in my mind. And then I began to talk.

A monologue ensued for another hour or more and then there was silence. I felt exhausted. I had told her everything, except for the bit that I had not reconciled myself to, the bit that was perhaps actually the reason behind this visit. The timing was perfect as Martha dealt the big blow. She asked a simple question, and it poured instant light on the inner darkness that had captured me and restrained me in many ways. My head was throbbing, or perhaps it was my heart. I felt my heart palpitating as I answered her question. My answer was a firm and simple no.

With that *no*, the pain broke loose; the dam collapsed. I could finally cut through the superficial stuff and speak about what really mattered. I shared things with this stranger that I had not told myself. I laid it all down and bared my soul to her.

Sometime later, I walked out of that room; truth had set in. As I made my way to the railway station, I surrendered my situation to my heavenly Father and asked Him to have His way with me—I had worn myself out, and I could not resist Him anymore.

Back in the warmth of my room at home in Vienna, sitting on my favorite couch, I lit a candle. Watching the candle burn, I offered my pain to God and healing began to take over. My meeting with Martha had indeed been a divine encounter!

WALKS OF LIFE

When two people enter into a relationship with each other, things happen. You may walk together over a lifetime or you may walk together for a season. The seasonal walks are the glorious parentheses in our life's journey; they mold us, define us, and strengthen us; they build us up; and sadly, many times, they pull us down too. Whatever else they may do, they surely add perspective and give us reasons to ask the deeper questions, those that go beyond our current existence here on earth and make the larger walk of life more significant.

Some walks only last for a couple of minutes, perhaps with a fellow traveler in a bus or on the street. A few words might be exchanged, but they hit you like a bolt of lightning; they leave their mark. And then some walks last long enough to establish a deep friendship.

Some walks help you attain or achieve something that you would never get without that circumstantial interaction. Then there are the celestial interactions with God Himself. These walks change the course of your life, and something so significant happens that it cannot be ignored anymore.

My interactions with Martha were of that nature. I met God Himself as I walked with Martha through some challenging and heartbreaking moments of my life. Over time, our profound interactions took us on journeys across two continents. Our hearts went on galactic adventures confronting truth and beauty in unfathomable ways, exposing and opening locked rooms that had been tucked away in the dark recesses of my heart.

TRUTH & BEAUTY

"Do we have to part?" asked Beauty, twirling to a tune.
She didn't't hear Truth, as He left the room.

Truth and Beauty met in the neighborhood.
He loved Beauty, but she never understood.

Beauty dwelt in meadows green and homes full of life,
where families looked perfect and hid all their strife.

But she couldn't resist Truth clad like a beggar,
for in His heart she found honey and nectar.

The rich tables overflowed with feast and wine,
but the fresh water at the spring just tasted divine.

Then one day, in the midst of coffee klatch with few,
Beauty heard her heart call out to Truth!

She said, "Everyone wants me and yearns for my company.
But the place I most desire, is to sit on Your knee!

"It's hard and cold and I feel exposed,
but Your arms enfold me; I am transposed.

"You take me through dark tunnels, with graffiti on walls.
Through gloomy forebodings, I hear wailing and howls.

"I hear You whisper deep within;
Your words haunt me, but I won't listen.

"I received Your invitation to a cup of tea;
I'm sorry, I chose rather to flee.

❁ ❁ ❁

❊ ❊ ❊

"The last time we met in the garden of Pain,
I felt calm and clean and elated again.

"Although I'm beautiful and desired by all,
they fall for the mask that so enthralls.

"For I feel no beauty within my bones.
I'm all dried up, haggard, and blown!"

Truth dwells in the bosom of maladies.
He puts on the lights where no one wants to see.

He touches where it hurts, the muddles and the tangles.
They need to be resolved; we must win those battles.

"Now I know what all that meant,
the wails and howls, petulance and lament.

"The wall with the graffiti was my heart.
No wonder Your presence made me want to depart.

"I have my answer now; I know I must choose,
Truth and Beauty, yes we can suffuse.

"Please take my heart, please be my Anchor.
Here I am, Truth, come let's dwell together.

"With You I feel content and free.
No pretense, I can just be.

"Your bosom is my home, my bastion.
You are my beauty, my true reflection!"

JACOB

Beauty's walk on quicksand begins with the inner hubbub when she confronts herself with Truth; the attraction is so strong, she can't resist Him. And it is not Truth that she resists. Beauty is resisting her own story; she is resisting dealing with her past, her unresolved identity. Those have been my struggles, as well. Perhaps we have all been in such a place. Truth is always compelling; it is daring, strong, bright, and beautiful but never fearful. Truth is worth choosing. Some of you like me may not have addressed the pain, the guilt, the rejections, the exploitations, and the assaults that we surrender ourselves to on our journeys. The adversities and the traumas that have impacted us continue to influence the choices we make; we choose to close those rooms and move on.

We distance ourselves and move on for so long that we do not recognize the source of those jolts of pain that come and go and leave their scars. And our loved ones are mostly at the receiving end of our pain. We ink our relationships with the color of our experiences. Intimate relationships reflect our souls. It is through these walks that we see the things hidden. It is precisely on these intimate journeys that we encounter Truth.

One summer evening, Jacob came over. We had known each other for many years and a healthy friendship had evolved. Our friendship found its roots in our common faith and belief in God. We were on the terrace above my flat; the sun was setting. It was a balmy evening, and the yellow and pink roses planted firm in the red soil were nodding gleefully around us. Even the vine creeping up the square columns seemed sprightly and elated. Summers in Vienna are always significant. It is that time of the year when my heart feels at home. The days were long and the starry nights were filled with music. The molten, golden color of dusk makes you feel secure and content. As this beautiful golden shade of dusk took over, we bent our heads in thanksgiving and reflection. Jacob looked up and smiled at me; it was so good to see him again. It had been a few years since we last spent time together on my terrace. He talked me through his story, through those years of trudging on quicksand that I had missed. Jacob began sharing "I had been resisting God for a long, long time. I don't know when the first disappointments in life set in and when I started blaming God for them. I didn't do it consciously, but I had estranged myself from Him over the years until I met Martha. Things began to happen, and I felt like God was shaking me and waking me up from a deep, deep slumber."

JACOB'S WRESTLE

That night Jacob got up and took his two wives, his two female servants and his eleven sons and crossed the ford of the Jabbok. After he had sent them across the stream, he sent over all his possessions. So Jacob was left alone; and a man wrestled with him until daybreak. When the man saw that he could not overpower him, he touched the socket of Jacob's hip so that his hip was wrenched as he wrestled with the man. Then the man said, "Let me go, for it is daybreak." But Jacob replied, "I will not let you go, unless you bless me." The man asked him, "What is your name?" "Jacob," he answered. Then the man said, "Your name will no longer be Jacob, but Israel, because you have struggled with God and with humans and have overcome." Jacob said, "Please tell me your name." But he replied, "Why do you ask my name?" Then he blessed him there. So Jacob called the place Peniel, saying, "It is because I saw God face to face, and yet my life was spared."

Genesis 32:22–30

JACOB'S STORY

Jacob drove the car to the edge of the woods. As he sat behind the wheel, he wasn't sure if he had come to the right place today. He had walked through these woods since childhood. It was home—a place where he had spent some of his finest hours. The soft bed of dry leaves had soaked up years of laughter and tears. He had experienced many seasons in these woods, seasons saturated with memories. The fiery autumn colors were nostalgic. It made him rub his hands with vigor, exhibiting his inane desire for the first snowfall. His heart leapt with delight as he imagined the light pat of falling snow outside his window, the fireplace with the crackling sound of wood, his beloved cherry brown leather couch that let him curl up and snuggle. The bamboo bowl, which he had picked up on one of his eastern voyages, stood on a delicate side table made of mahogany. Warm, crunchy nuts of all shapes and sizes filled the bowl to the brim, and an exquisite decanter of deep red oak wine stood next to it. It was picture perfect, and Leah had always been a part of it.

His deep breathing whispered wretchedness and sorrow, as he decidedly stepped out of the car and went into the woods. She was a city girl and didn't enjoy the woods as much as he did. This had been his hiding place. But this day was like none other. High tides of pain overtook him. The pain kept getting stronger, and the tides kept coming along with the ugly flashes of stormy debates with his wife, which had gone out of control on many occasions. He tried to confront those hideous images, but they produced further despair.

He walked down into the woods and reached the spot of silence. Deep in the woods, Jacob had discovered a grove of Austrian pine trees that stood in a natural circle of sorts. He had often spread his light air mattress on the floor of the forest there and had spent hours lying down, watching bits of blue sky with streams of golden light seeping through little notches between the heavily laden green branches. There were days in summer when he had spent hours at this very spot, sometimes in Leah's company. The play of lights as the day traveled toward dusk had absorbed her as well.

It all felt strange. It was autumn. Flaming red and golden leaves fell onto the floor of the forest in a beautiful rhythm struck by the cold wind. Jacob stood transfixed in the center of that circle like he had always done, but there was no elation. He felt feelings of dread, deep despair, anguish, and bitterness grip at his heart. Jacob encountered his first panic attack. And he fought. It was to be his first night of wrestling.

THE JOURNEY OF PAIN

Jacob had grown in the midst of mountains in Austria—the beautiful land of mountains and rivers, fields and cathedrals, castles and vineyards, breathtaking lakes, whispering forests, and snow-clad glaciers. It is indeed a slice of heaven on earth. Jacob loved his country. He had spent a lot of time in the mountains in tough terrain and had all the modern paraphernalia that one needed to have a comfortable stay in such whereabouts.

Jacob fought the panic attack that was making him breathless; he decided to spend the night in his spot of silence. Rushing back to the car, he got out his gear for the night and dragged it along to his spot.

He pulled out his cheese sandwich and munched introspectively between sips of sweet apple juice. Then he got into his sleeping bag and lay down in the spot of silence. As the lights changed in the evening sky, spreading a red fiery hue over the forest, the tears began to roll. It had been a long, hard journey. Leah and Jacob had been together in high school and had started dating each other in their teens. He had known, even then, that he would marry her someday. It was surreal. The sureness had baffled and mystified him at times. He proposed to her on her twenty-first birthday, and she said yes. They married a couple of years later and had four wonderful kids.

After the children were born, Leah and Jacob had very little time for each other, each caught up in his or her own world until it became difficult to relate to the person who had meant everything to them not so long ago. They had separated for a while, hoping that some distance would add perspective, and they would find a way to sort out their differences. But the separation did not work. Leah fell in love with another man during this phase of their separation.

How could she have done it? How could Leah have betrayed him so? How could she have fallen for another? Could she not have chosen another day to leave him? Had she forgotten their fifteenth wedding anniversary? He had missed many of them himself and had wanted to make it up to her for the years that went by in oblivion. Jacob had booked a holiday to Patagonia for Leah and himself. They would start off from Argentina and drive through Patagonia into Chile. Leah had wanted to visit the glacial lakes strewn with icebergs for many years now. However, she had not been herself lately. She greeted him each evening when he scrambled in from work with a weak, forlorn smile, but he had shrugged it off. He had shrugged off far too much over the years, and now it was time to wrestle with it all.

Jacob woke up early the next morning. The day was dawning and sunrise stood around the corner. All of it was so familiar—the sounds, the scent, and the colors of dawn. This used to be his comfort zone. He had come here last evening to seek solace and have his pain alleviated. He felt nothing of the sort. It was brutal. A time of enormous pain was upon him, pain that would help clear the fog of pretense in which he had engulfed himself in his quest to live yet another day in freedom. In his insatiable quest for freedom, he had sold himself to what enslaves. Jacob packed his rucksack and moved on. He left the spot of silence.

He had a plan, and he was determined to win Leah back. Jacob's efforts did not succeed and Leah divorced Jacob a year later. It took years, however, for Jacob to let Leah go. He carried her with him and let her memories dictate his life. She was an integral part of his life now that she was away, and she influenced all his decisions. He had never been so dependent on her when they were together. But now it all seemed to matter. What would Leah have chosen for the kitchen window? How would she have cooked the turkey at Christmas? Would she want their youngest son to study in a private school? Jacob isolated himself and spent long hours in the office. He shut himself in his office even on weekends. If ever an opportunity presented itself to make a new friend, Jacob ran away, especially if it was a woman. He felt like he was betraying Leah, although Leah had moved on. She had resettled with another man.

Time went by. Jacob had frozen his feelings for ten long years since that awful day when Leah had asked him for a divorce. One early autumn morning, Jacob woke up struggling in bed. The bed sheet was soaked in sweat. He seemed to have been in the midst of a physical encounter with a person of gigantic proportions. Actually, Jacob had been wrapped up in a king-sized palm in a very tight grip. The pain was agonizing, but at the same time Jacob felt strangely heartened! He cried out in distress. The palm softened its grip momentarily. Jacob tried to run, but the palm held him captive again! And it seemed to go on. Jacob resisted and struggled until it woke him up.

He sat on the edge of his bed wondering if the Man in the dream had been his own father. He had not seen the Man, of course, but the palm and the hand had been masculine. Jacob had never really had a father figure in his life. His father had deserted the family when he was twelve years old. He was raised by his mother in a household that was predominantly female. He had three sisters. Yet something unearthly had happened in that dream. Something impalpable, but Jacob knew it to be true, as true as his breathing that was very heavy that morning. Jacob wrestled all day in his office trying to get those images out of his head. Yet he desired to see the face of the Man Who had gripped him so tightly in His king-sized palm.

PAIN SURRENDERS

It was six o'clock in the evening. Jacob walked out of his office with his shoulders drooped. It had been a tough day. Leah and Jacob had separated ten years ago, and he found it difficult to rationally evaluate his life. A decade had been devoted to the memories of Leah; they had paralyzed him. Then there was the dream he had early this morning. Who was that Man who had gripped him so tightly in his palm? He had never been held in that strange manner before; the palm was so big, it had felt like the warm chest of a Man. It had been more than a tight grip. His lungs had gasped for air, and even through the ordeal he had felt new life breathe into him. It was hard to make sense of it all. This dream could not have been better timed. Over the next few days, Jacob felt a sense of excitement run through his veins; he could not explain it.

He was standing at a popular crossing on Ringstrasse in the city center waiting for the light to turn green. Directly opposite him stood Vienna's famous opera house, one of Vienna's opulent and majestic monuments. He had never been a fan of opera, but he found himself walking to the ticket counter. The famous *La Traviata* was being performed tonight, and Jacob bought himself a ticket. As he entered through the main lobby, he held his breath at the sheer beauty of the gorgeous Schwind-Foyer, the Frescoes, and the central staircase itself. For those of you who may care to know, the Schwind-Foyer is named after a famous painter called Moritz von Schwind. Sixteen of his oil paintings hang in this foyer. This beautiful building had first opened its doors in 1869 with Mozart's, *Don Juan* in the majestic presence of Emperor Franz Josef and his beautiful wife, Queen Elizabeth. Jacob was fascinated by the extravaganza that evening. Men and women all showed up in elegant evening wear, walking with poise and a certain air that naturally overtakes you when you walk in such interiors. You feel a part of royalty yourself.

La Traviata literally means, "the fallen woman." Jacob had not prepared himself for the opera. He did not know the story. The three acts revolve around the lady, Violetta Valery, who is a famed courtesan. At one of her lavish parties, she meets Alfredo Germont, a man who has loved her from afar while Violetta has been conducting an affair of her own with the Baron Douphol. Violetta gets to hear from the common grapevine about Alfredo's feelings. She is flattered and begins contemplating if Alfredo indeed is the man for her. As time moves on, Violetta falls deeply in love with Alfredo and changes her old ways. She moves in with Alfredo and lives a life devoid of all the past debaucheries and reckless friendships. Alfredo has now become the reason of her existence. This is the story of Violetta who separates from her beloved and finally meets him at the climax when she is besieged by a deadly illness and moments away from death's beckoning.

Jacob was moved by the opera. It had spoken into his wounds. When he got home he poured himself a brandy and settled down cozily on his favorite cherry brown leather couch. His maid Hilda had gotten the fireplace going in time, and his library was pleasantly warm. As he moved the brandy snifter between his fingers, meditatively watching the golden honey liquid swirl, he felt the first pangs of hunger again. Hunger not for food, but for life. Jacob walked to the mammoth bookshelf made out of chestnut wood and began frantically searching and flipping through the neat rows of books, until at last he found what he had been looking for. It was a Bible. A silver-leafed Bible bound in a deep blue leather cover. He opened it casually and began leafing through the pages, working out of distant memory, searching feverishly until his eyes fell on the words, "I am your shield, your exceedingly great reward." It was from the book of Genesis, the book of beginnings. Those words were the beginning of a promise God made to Abraham. Abraham and Sarah were married; they were old and they could not have children. When everything seemed lost and meaningless with old age, God spoke to Abraham in a vision. God seemed to be shaking Abraham up and pacifying him in superlative terminology. "I am your reward, your super reward, your exceedingly much reward!"

Those words engrossed Jacob through the night. He had been seven years old when his mother shared the story of Abraham, Isaac, and Jacob with him. The stories of these three men with God had fascinated him. God had been real to them. He was someone whom they spoke with, shared their feelings, secrets, and desires with.

Jacob reminisced about a late summer experience; he had been walking with his mother through the forest together, picking up wildflowers and pieces of scented wood. His mother was sitting on the floor of the forest and reading. Jacob loved it when she read out loud to him. It provided him with space to dream and imagine things that were so alienated from his day-to-day life. She read out loud,

That night Jacob got up and took his two wives, his two female servants and his eleven sons and crossed the ford of the Jabbok. After he had sent them across the stream, he sent over all his possessions. So Jacob was left alone, and a man wrestled with him till daybreak. When the man saw that he could not overpower him, he touched the socket of Jacob's hip so that his hip was wrenched as he wrestled with the man. Then the man said, "Let me go, for it is daybreak." But Jacob replied, "I will not let you go unless you bless me." The man asked him, "What is your name?" "Jacob," he answered. Then the man said, "Your name will no longer be Jacob, but Israel, because you have struggled with God and with humans and have overcome." Jacob said, "Please tell me your name." But he replied, "Why do you ask my name?" Then he blessed him there. So Jacob called the place Peniel, saying, "It is because I saw God face to face, and yet my life was spared."

Genesis 32:22–30

This story had fascinated Jacob endlessly, not just because he shared the same name. Jacob had often wondered then, *What does God look like? Why did God wrestle with Jacob and break his hip? Were they playing with each other?* It had been way beyond his comprehension as a child, and he now remembered his mother's words of advice: "As you keep growing older, my son, you will wrestle with many things, with friends, family, and situations. There will be many challenges that come your way, but just like in this story, do not let go of God until He has blessed you. It may seem like He is hurting you. Your hip may be broken too with the weight of your sufferings and trials, but do not resist Him; do not let go of God. He is your Healer. He heals the brokenhearted and binds up their wounds."

MOVING ON

Jacob went to bed with his Bible spread across his chest that night. Morning ushered in a new day, and Jacob woke up wondering if he had dreamed again until his eyes fell upon the Bible lying on his bed. He stepped out onto the veranda. It was fresh and autumn had truly set in. He gazed at the beautiful pine trees that were spread on the tiny slopes around his house, as if noticing them for the first time. Hilda came in unannounced with her chirpy, "Guten Morgen, Jacob!" and a tray laden with fresh coffee and large, thick slices of poppy seed cake. As he sipped his coffee sitting on the ledge, he felt good. He spoke those lines aloud, the lines that God had spoken to Abraham: "Fear not, Abram: I am thy shield, and thy exceeding great reward" (Genesis 15:1, KJV). Jacob wanted to talk. He wanted to connect with the God of his childhood, but he was out of practice. He bit into the slice of poppy seed cake and scrolled through his cell phone, noting his appointments for the day, and hurried back into his room.

He would soon be on his way to meet Martha. He had heard of Martha a couple of years ago, from his colleague Lucy. Lucy had been on the verge of a divorce, and she had received counseling from Martha. Lucy's recommendations had always been priceless. Jacob had fixed an appointment with Martha a month ago; he did not know what to expect, but he decided to take the chance. Since he had a business trip planned in Melk, and Martha had her counseling practice twice each month in this beautiful town, he planned to stay an extra night and give the counseling session a try.

Jacob's drive from Vienna to Melk was a quiet one. He loved long drives, listening to classical music, and enjoying his favorite countryside. The journey to Melk, however, was mainly on the highway. He switched on his music system. Bach's "Goldberg Variations" began to play. Leah had loved this piece of music performed by Glenn Gould, but his thoughts soon came back to the present. The meeting that lay in front of him would be a first of sorts. He had never been to a counselor before, and he had no clue what to expect. He found himself driving to his destination with an optimism that had long evaded him. He had tried talking to God the night before, but it sounded surreal. *"Are you really out there God? Do you hear me? Was it you that gripped me so tight in the palm of your hand that night? Why? Do you really care? Then please come get me out of this mess."* Again and again he spoke to the Lord of his childhood as he kept driving. He invited God to come and settle the scores, to wipe the tears, to give him back his dignity, his life, his joy, and even as he spoke to God, he sensed peace on the horizon.

Melk is a pretty little town on the Danube River, well known for its abbey, "Stift Melk." A town with character and history, it is home to the Benedictine monks who inherited a castle from Leopold II in the year 1089, which then came to be known as the Melk Abbey. It has one of the most impressive libraries that came into being in the twelfth century, a huge hall with marble flooring, and high ceilings painted with beautiful frescoes. It has an air of purity and beauty that makes you want to hang in there for hours on end, just to soak in the atmosphere and watch people come in and slip out, including the Benedictine monks in their black robes looking mysterious and unapproachable. The vast Abbey Park provides you with wonderful views of the Danube with boats carrying happy tourists sailing across at a leisurely pace.

Jacob parked his car, picked up a coffee from a stall nearby, and walked through Abbey Park. He arrived at the riverbank and sat down on the cemented stairs. The Danube is a beautiful river. It does get violent at times, flooding towns and destroying crops, but it is mostly calm and beckoning, like it was this morning. There was another hour to go before his appointment, so Jacob decided to spend it here. He tried to prepare himself for the questions that would come. It felt like a thick fog was coming in and pervading the inner recesses of his mind, and he could not think clearly. He had not smoked in years, but when he picked up his coffee at the stall, he had impulsively bought a pack. Jacob lit a cigarette and inhaled a few drags. He didn't like it. Stubbing it out, he stood up and unwittingly patted his rear to kick off any dirt that may have hung on to his jeans from the cemented stairs. He took one last look across the river at the reeds growing on the green Danube Delta with groves of willow trees further behind, inhaled deeply, and walked decisively toward Martha's office a few blocks away.

THE INNER ROOM

Martha had been waiting for Jacob at the entrance of a tiny chapel in a smaller abbey where she had her practice. This first meeting then led to a series of meetings between them in Salzburg and Melk over the next twelve months. The interactions with Martha were initially exhaustive and cumbersome. Confronting and owning up is never easy. We dread to step into that inner room that exists in each of us. The room where we stack up things, people, experiences, disappointments, dejections, rejections, and all things reprehensible; they are stacked away but never thrown out. We lock it all up, lest it hinders our today. But these are the very things that define us and create a roadblock, that paralyze the chords of our hearts. God gave us these chords, which are meant to be united with other chords to make melodies, wipe tears, give hugs, share sorrows, and multiply joy. But it stops happening. We abstain. We freeze. We need God to get a grip on us, and He will, if only we allow Him to.

Jacob finally took that crucial step. He unlocked the door to the inner room of his heart. He opened up the windows and aired it out. He let the sun in. Today that room has turned into a beautiful garden where others find space, love, solace, and comfort. We cannot give unless we receive. And we cannot receive enough from human resources. We need to tap the supernatural source—a God Who has no beginning and no end. A God Who loves passionately without conditions. He may rebuke you, get a tight grip on you, shake you up a bit every now and then, but He will never stop giving. He never stops loving. He is a generous God, a loving Father. Jacob went to the source of life and found all that he had lost. God has now become his everlasting reward. Jacob is alive again. He has truly moved on.

Before we can be cured we must want to be cured. Those who really wish for help will get it; but for many modern people even the wish is difficult.

C. S. Lewis, *Mere Christianity*

WHAT QUALIFIES MARTHA?

Martha has been working as a counselor for over twenty-five years now. She has helped hundreds of hurting men and women in Austria and Germany to fix what is broken, to walk in freedom with confidence and renewed strength and rebuild their lives. She is often invited to speak at various seminars and workshops, at churches, and at conferences. When Martha steps up on stage, she is simply introduced as Martha Schubert. No reading out of all her varied degrees or accomplishments. That impresses me. She concerns herself with matters of the heart. Her passionate desire is to be an instrument through which hurting and broken people can find the healing power of God's presence in their own lives.

Martha is a trained Christian counselor with a degree in supervision and counseling. Academic qualifications are important, but answering the Call is more significant. When we answer the Call, God qualifies us and equips us in His own distinct way. Our academic qualifications are mere tools that God uses. It is the sensitivity that God has placed in your heart through your own experiences that enables Him to do extraordinary things through you, things that the best of academic qualifications, on their own, would not achieve. A supernatural calling drives you to be an instrument for God's purposes.

The training in God's school begins much earlier, way before you hear the Call. It begins through the lessons of life. We are taught the hard way many times, through tough, heartbreaking experiences. Unless we ourselves experience pain and suffering in varied degrees, we cannot comfort another. A victim of rape and assault can best empathize with another who has experienced something similar. Many may call themselves counselors, but without God's input, at best, they can only sympathize. They may cure the ailments, but they cannot renew your mind or give you a new life; that is something only the Creator can do with His created beings.

The story of the prophet Elijah from the Old Testament in the Bible fascinates me. He was called to prophesy and minister in Israel, but his training period consisted of "small" jobs, like going and looking after the widow and her son, and for a few years at that! That is all that God commanded him to do at one point in time in his journey, and he did it faithfully. You can read about the outcome in the book of 1 Kings in the Bible.

Martha had a sad story too. She had painful and extreme experiences during the tender, formative years of her life, experiences that many of us may have been spared from. It could have all gone the wrong way for her. She did not see the purpose in continuing to live in a world where she had been unjustly treated, mishandled, and unloved. Martha let God teach her through her pain. He prepared her in a manner that no school could have. She allowed Him to show her His eternal perspective. He called and she followed. Her own healing began as she offered herself to be used by God to reach out and heal others.

Brothers and sisters, think of what you were when you were called. Not many of you were wise by human standards; not many were influential; not many were of noble birth. But God chose the foolish things of the world to shame the wise; God chose the weak things of the world to shame the strong. God chose the lowly things of this world and the despised things —and the things that are not —to nullify the things that are, so that no one may boast before him.

1 Corinthians 1:26–29

WHAT ARE WE SEEKING?
A REVELATION OR AN ENCOUNTER?

I've often heard and read that we need to be at the very end of ourselves—weak and broken, humble and seeking—in order that God may reveal Himself to us. It makes me wonder about God's personality. Does He derive pleasure out of our brokenness? He certainly has many ways and means of revealing Himself and He does so. The earth and the universe itself announce His majestic existence.

But I think it is quite another matter altogether to have an encounter with God. We must want it. Whatever drives us to that point, ecstasy or pain, we must want it. "God says, 'Come!' And let the one who hears say, 'Come!' Let the one who is thirsty come; and let the one who wishes take the free gift of the water of life" (Revelation 22:17). We need to thirst for the liquid that sustains life, that drives it and makes each day meaningful and worth living. Some of us are so overwhelmed with God that we shy away from wanting to know more. He seems to be someone Who is much beyond our reach. We train ourselves to believe that God lives in a world that is so alien, so distant, that He simply cannot penetrate into our world, even if He wanted to. It is the infidelity of our own minds, our ego, and our fears that stop us from encountering a God Who is very personal, very intimate, very seeking. The possibility of having Him intervene into our small and private lives unnerves us. What stops us? Why would we not want to meet this Daddy God Who created us? He is a God Who watches over us, Who seeks us, and Who wants us.

One of the first prayers that my mother taught me as a little girl was the Lord's Prayer. I prayed that prayer with wholeheartedness, although I didn't really think of God as my heavenly Father then, not in the "daddy" sense, for a very long time. Not until I learned to talk to Him with my very own vocabulary of tears, with the vocabulary of a bruised and a broken heart, with the words of a desperate and lonely soul. It was through those desolate years that I learned to talk to Him, and He became my very own "Daddy God."

Our capacity to see and hear things that we normally cannot—to experience and feel love—heightens when we are broken. The ragged edge of our lives leaves us with an option to wither away or to discover the dark spaces that we have vehemently ignored in our innate desire to stay steady, to do what needs to be done, to be all that we are expected to be, and to let the show go on. We decide on the course, and we control the navigation channels of our lives. We believe we own ourselves. We plan the best we can, stock our boat with provisions, and prepare ourselves for every possible calamity that we can think of. We have laid the carpets on the deck and spread our identities all over our boat. But all it takes is a hairline crack in the wood underneath the carpet. The split expands and it turns into a hole of mammoth proportions. A situation we cannot handle enfolds around us, and it is exactly through one such split, when you are desolate and weary, where you may have the privilege of encountering the living God!

I am often astounded at the varied ways in which God equips us to encounter Him. After all, it is not a matter of meeting a friend who lives next door or in another country. He is the Supreme Force, the Commander of the angel armies, the One Who holds the entire universe in the palm of His hands. He chooses to make Himself accessible to you and me. We need to have a deep, strong desire to meet Him, to experience Him, and to have an encounter with Him. This desire needs to stem out of the very depths of our soul. Those are the qualifiers. And even then, there is no guarantee. We do not have a contract with Him, and we certainly cannot bargain with the Alpha and the Omega.

Sometimes this searching and seeking leads us to transcendental experiences, but that does not necessarily mean that we have encountered God. Those experiences need to be put to the test. Do they have the capacity to lift you up when your life collapses all around you? Do those mystical experiences heal you? Do they save you, restore you, and renew you?

We cannot second-guess God, but He can read our very thoughts, even before they are conceived.

You have searched me, Lord, and you know me. You know when I sit and when I rise; you perceive my thoughts from afar. You discern my going out and my lying down; you are familiar with all my ways. Before a word is on my tongue you, Lord, know it completely.

Psalm 139:1–4

UNENDING PAIN, UNENDING HEALING

They told me that Pain won't stay.
Just a little longer, then it goes away.
I trusted and waited, till I saw the joke,
Pain never goes away, your arteries it chokes.
And what's more, an astounded me discovered;
it has its moods and shades, it leaves you battered!

Pain rained on me, like the Mumbai monsoon.
It was gray and dark; I smelled sadness and gloom.
And wonder of wonders, none of them saw —
my friends and foes, the birds and the willows.
I couldn't blame them; it was the wall of smiles
that I'd built over years, it ran into miles.

Then Healing appeared out of nowhere one day.
He saw through my smiles; the tears broke the bay.
Pain never ends, it comes visiting on jaunts;
don't try to predict its wailings and haunts.
Let it not define you or make you or break you.
There is a balm for every wound, please let God heal you!

For unending pain, there is unending healing.
March on, fellow traveler, the crown is waiting!

PAIN

Pain has often bewildered me. I have experienced it in many forms since childhood. I often imagined a world without pain, what would it be like. As a twenty-one year old who lost her mom in a sudden, tragic event, I thought I would die, not just out of grief but out of pain. We experience pain through the physical and emotional realm. I haven't been spared the physical pains either, from growing-up pains to severe hemorrhages that finally took me to the surgical ward.

The good-byes and farewells, the constant comings and goings of people in my life was painful too. Having grown up in a country like India, the poverty, the hunger, the corruption, and the negligence leaves its marks on you. It hurts. But a lot of good has come out of this very pain. It makes you sensitive and fills you with love and compassion for those who are going through similar events in their lives. You are able to lend a shoulder and gather the tears of someone in pain. That is a privilege. My relationship with God began through the throes of pain, and I can't imagine life without Him.

But many of us do not really deal with pain. We accept it as life's reality and it is, but it has its consequences. It does not leave us unchanged. It matters what you do with your pain. People like Martha dedicate their lives to helping the hurt and wounded. They counsel and mentor in a manner in which we learn to connect and address all our grievances to God. He is the almighty Healer and Counselor. He is a God Who does not ignore pain. He has legitimized it by stepping into the realm of time, becoming Man, a suffering Servant Who died on the cross to pay the price for you and me, to set us free from the clutches of sin, pain, and condemnation.

What makes Martha so special? Why is she qualified to touch and participate in the wounds and pains of others? Why do women and men, young and old, feel comfortable relating life's lurid wounds on their bodies and souls with Martha? If you have been wounded, you are qualified to help another heal. You may not be called to dedicate your life to this cause, but you and I are certainly called to take a moment and look over our shoulders as we go about our day-to-day lives. We are called to reach out to that someone whom we may not personally know, a colleague or a fellow traveler perhaps. It does take a lot to reach out to someone you do not know but are sharing time and space with on a journey, in an office, or even at a café. Yes, it does take a lot but in reaching out, you transform yourself into a golden vessel for God's own use. It is worth it.

I salute Martha! She walks on quicksand each day. She is called to hurt for, and with, others, to offer love and advice, to counsel, and to lovingly point to the source of all healing — God.

Dismiss me not thy service Lord,
But train me for thy will;
For even I in fields so broad
Some duties may fulfill;
And I will ask for no reward,
Except to serve thee still.
Our Master all the work has done,
He asks for us to-day;
Sharing His service everyone
Share too His Sonship may.
Lord I would serve and be a son;
Dismiss me not, I pray.

Thomas T. Lynch[2]

---

[2] Thomas T. Lynch, excerpts from the hymn, "Dismiss Me Not Thy Service, Lord," 1855, public domain.

PART 4: STAR SAPPHIRE

STAR SAPPHIRE

God numbered all the stars; He gave them all their names.
Not one goes missing; He has set them in their place.

And some He has set, on the earth below,
they shine in dark alleys, they expose the foe.

Many such beacons on the planet there are;
one such I met, a sapphire star.

His focus, zeal, and hunger for truth.
His home, his folk, his neighborhood.

He shepherds and leads them like his very own.
Family is not by blood alone.

He has taken the message to many he does not know.
His sapphire awaits him, and much more is in store.

In Josiah, I have found a brother who keeps it all so simple. He has inspired me through his writings and the manner in which he conducts his day-to-day life. Jesus has called us to love our neighbors as ourselves.

Josiah is a fine example of a person who truly endeavors to do so. There is nothing as challenging and humbling as to love your neighbor as yourself. Whatever else we may choose to do with our lives, we are all called to this common purpose.

His love for Christ is absolutely infectious! He is my star sapphire.

LONDON CALLING

Josiah is a fifty-eight year old man; he lives in a cute little house on the eastern outskirts of London with his beautiful wife, Mary, and their angelic daughter, Beth. It is the sort of family that you usually meet in a fairy tale. A small yet powerful pack of three they are! And I can't remember a time when I have seen them apart.

Josiah's walk has touched me and inspired me. It has defined many a life-changing moment. I met Josiah in the summer of 2002. A small group of locals were meeting to do a Bible study in my sister's neighborhood. I had been to London on a holiday in 1993, but this time around, it was a family visit. My sister had recently settled there with her husband.

I had been most amazed by the generosity bestowed upon my sister in the form of a pretty little London flat in the affluent north-eastern suburb of Buckhurst Hill. Buckhurst Hill was interestingly also called Bucket Hill at one point in time—a hill covered with beech trees. However, I do not see the connection between beech trees and buckets! That was around the year 1135 when Buckhurst Hill lay in the Epping Forest, scattered with a few houses along the ancient road from Woodford to Loughton. It is at the western edge of Essex and can be easily reached now with the London Underground.

I wanted to meet the people who had come to care deeply for Janis within a couple of weeks of knowing her. They cared enough so as to inconvenience themselves and make it possible to let Janis have an apartment, rent free. As she gushed and told me the story over the phone, I knew I wanted to meet her new friends. The events that had happened in her life were indeed extraordinary. I had never experienced this level of neighborly generosity, and I wanted to see it for myself.

THE PRETTY LITTLE FLAT AT BUCKHURST HILL

Ireached London on a lovely summer afternoon. My sister and brother-in-law picked me up at the airport. It had been a long journey from home, but I felt fresh with excitement! After all, a lot of new experiences awaited me and I couldn't wait to get started.

The apartment at Buckhurst Hill where my sister lived was magical. Small, cute, inviting, and enchanting! The most important room in a house has always been the kitchen, for me. So that's where I headed first. It was a tiny, well-equipped, sunny little kitchen. My eyes fell on a colorful, miniature garden gnome sitting happily on the refrigerator. My sister tapped him gently on the head and he began merrily singing, "Da di da dum dum di day!" I loved this apartment and felt at home immediately.

I soon learned that the beautiful apartment given to my sister was not only an act of generosity. The owner had actually moved into his friend's home in order to make his flat available for Janis. I was to meet my sister's fairy godfather in a couple of hours on that very day. His name was Joe. When he arrived, he walked in with a cheerful, shy grin and headed right to the bathroom to do some repair work! He turned out to be a genuine, warm-hearted man with an extraordinarily generous heart.

Too much had happened on my very first day in London, and as I went to bed that night, I found it difficult to fall asleep. My thoughts wandered to the events of the day and to Janis' new friends: a modest group of people, some families, a few singles, and a pretty little angelic child in their midst. I listened in to their stories, felt their concern and love for each other, and visited one of their homes. I decided that I liked them. They were simply authentic and it made me wonder, *What in the world drove these simple folk to do enormous deeds of self-sacrifice toward strangers?*

THE MEETING

My sister, Janis, introduced me to Josiah and his wife, Mary. Their lovely daughter, Beth, was about three years old then. Their home was a lovely little house on a curvy street, lined up with pretty Georgian-styled houses with perfectly manicured garden patches, some big enough to contain a swimming pool. I loved the setting. It reminded me of my favorite books that I read in my childhood, books that described this beautiful country. Enid Blyton was one of my favorite authors, and each time I read a *Famous Five Adventure*, I would dream of visiting England. She had managed to make it personal and familiar for me. Some of the neighboring gardens had picket fences; these were British gardens indeed. The lawns were impeccably mowed, and the grass was bright, shiny green, and even all over. Daisies, daffodils, lavender, apple blossoms, cherry blossoms, bluebells, and camellias greeted me with gentle nods; these gardens were wooing me for attention.

Josiah's home had a warm, cozy feel about it. It was full up that late afternoon as we arrived. Some folk had made themselves comfortable on the carpeted floor. I was offered a nice little corner on a white couch that sunk in with a light *puff* sound effect as I sat myself down.

My sister had carefully informed me about the itinerary in advance; it would be a prayer meeting followed by some snacks and tea. This would be a new experience, and I went in with an open mind. Some of my childhood experiences at such meetings had been far from pleasant, and I secretly dreaded that it would be "ritualistic," a word that I had developed quite an allergy for over the years.

The meeting turned out to be far from ritualistic to my relief! No pretension, no sitting in pious attitude for hours on end, no feeling of being in the midst of superficial saints! These people just spoke their hearts out to God in an earnest manner that was very refreshing. They were truly conversing with the Creator of the universe. Their heads may not have been bent but their hearts were. I sensed and felt accepted not just by these folk but by God Himself. It brought back memories of my earlier walk with God, the time when I had knelt down in a small chapel and had given my heart to Jesus. I had fallen in love with Him. A passionate walk ensued with Him during those early years, but my relationship with Jesus succumbed to the trials of time.

KNIGHT IN SHINING ARMOR

My walk with the Lord had begun when I was sixteen. I studied in a convent school and a dear neighbor introduced me to the Bible one fine day. I had seen the Bible at church before, but the solemn manner in which these black leather-cased books were placed in specially made slots in the pews sent a "touch me not" signal through my veins. I felt it to be an unfriendly sort of book that was somehow not meant for a naughty child like me.

But when I began reading the Bible in earnest, it had a contradictory impact. The God I met in the Bible seemed very different from the one I had conjured up from my experiences thus far. Here was a God that I desired to know. He seemed to be the Knight in shining armor that every girl dreams of encountering. Someone who comes and scoops her out of distress, lifts her gently onto his horse, and rides off with her to a faraway land that's full of promise and hope.

> *When I was a little girl, my mama used to lock me in the attic when I was bad, which was pretty often, and I would . . . I would pretend I was a princess trapped in the tower by a wicked queen, and then suddenly this knight on a white horse with these colors flying would come charging up and draw his sword, and I would wave, and he would climb up the tower and rescue me.*

Film: *Pretty Woman*

One fine day, I went to church with my friendly neighbor. Over the few months that I had spent reading God's Word, I fell in love with Jesus, my Knight. I got down on my knees in the chapel, and I submitted my life to Him; I told Him I would be His forever. I trusted Him and I believed that He would come on His horse and rescue me when I needed it.

THE DARK SUMMERS

The day of distress did dawn when I was around twenty-one years old. My mother succumbed to her wounds in the hospital and ceased to exist. I desperately called out to the Knight in shining armor, the God of my Bible. I called out to Jesus! I needed to be rescued, but He didn't show up. My faith was inadequate, weak, and flummoxed. I could not sense His presence in the least! My eyes were swollen with tears, and my head was throbbing with the sudden vacuum that enveloped me. I could barely articulate words, and my heart threatened to explode. I deserted and ran away as far as I possibly could from my Knight; I did not want to analyze, I did not want to know, I asked no questions. I submitted myself to the seventh wave of pain, and it washed me onto the shore of pirate islands. I lived, I worked, I achieved, and made many friends, but I was not alive. It felt like a surreal life. At times, I would wake up as though from a deep slumber, but I ran like a flash, back into the mundane darkness and enslaved myself to all that glittered but wasn't really gold.

I sensed, however, that through those pain-filled years, this Knight in shining armor had never left my side. When things got overwhelming, I cried out to Him, and He answered, but He never explained why He had taken my mother away from me. The bond had disconnected but was not severed. How could it? It's a bond of blood. He would not let me escape. I had simply run away from home for a while. It's been a long chase. I ran for my life and in the process left it far behind. I had yearned for truth, but I embraced its illusion. That was as much as I could handle then, until the next dark dawn struck.

I was on an assignment in Hong Kong. This had been my first trip outside of India, and everything seemed to capture my fascination. From the malls and the high-rises, the spectacular lights that adorned the skyscrapers in the evening giving the city a bejeweled look, it felt like the very stars of heaven had descended to abide on these skyscrapers. I lived out of a tiny hotel room with a magnificent view. The Victoria Harbor glittered in the afternoon sun, the large glass windows in the room didn't seem to exist, and I felt transported to the bed of the glimmering waters each time I took in that view.

I had perched myself on the window sill and had been taking in this endless expanse of blue in front of me, mindlessly digging into my Kentucky Fried Chicken bucket and nibbling away at the crispy chicken chunks, which I had recently discovered. It was one of those moments when you feel content, and you don't really know why. However, those blissful moments at the window sill were broken into as the telephone rang. My sister lay in a hospital in India; she had been diagnosed with brain fever. The virus had affected her cerebellum, and Janis had lost her ability to control her body movements. She was in the intensive care unit, totally incapacitated. I took the first flight back to India. The fear of loss surfaced and gripped me all over again through those long days as my sister lay on her hospital bed. The city's best doctors were attending to her, but they gave us no reason whatsoever to be hopeful. That finally broke me down.

The monsoon season in Mumbai had advanced, and the month of June opened up old wounds. Although it had been seven years since I lost my mother, the pain constricted my limbs every June as the monsoons set in and brought back those fearful memories of loss and pain.

It was around seven in the evening, and I had been cooking some food for Dad who had to be relieved from his duty at the hospital. He watched over my sister during the day, and I kept vigil at night. My dear friend Melanie had given me her apartment, which was near the hospital. She was traveling and did not need it for a while. It was a stormy evening. The windows rattled relentlessly as a powerful breeze from the ocean swept through the land and brought with it weighty raindrops that the city really needed. I stood in the kitchen near the gas stove, ruminating and yet quite unfeeling, when a sudden spray of stormy rain water flew in through the window drenching me, waking me up from my spiritual slumber.

HEARTWRENCHING PRAYER

The spray of water that jetted from the window that June evening in 1996 opened up the plugs of my heart. I knelt on the ground and cried out all the losses of my life. I cried out my fears. I cried out the frustrations and the hurt. I cried out the pain. I cried out my entire struggle since that fateful day in 1988 when I lost my mother. I cried it all out. I felt that the God of my childhood was listening to me. He was gathering my tears. "Jesus!" I managed to cry out at last. I called out His name from the deep clandestine spaces that I had locked up within my being.

My sister began recovering within a fortnight and left the hospital after a couple of weeks. One morning the doctor walked in for his regular checkup on Janis. He came along with a bunch of eager medical interns and took them through Janis' medical history. I hung around in the room as discreetly as I possibly could. I knew it was class time and a very important lesson was being shared here. As the doctor came to the end of his lecture, a young lady asked him, "And Doctor, what do you think changed this life-threatening situation?" The doctor turned his head in my direction and replied, "This here is a miracle of love."

I agree it was indeed a miracle of love, but it was not my love that healed my sister from a life-threatening situation. It was God's love for her, for me. God's love for the both of us.

The Bible says that God has placed eternity in our hearts, and yet we can't understand Him and His ways with us. But we do know when we have had a supernatural encounter. It may come in the form of a new birth in the family, sometimes we encounter these eternal moments in a smile, and sometimes through life-saving miracles. These eternal encounters do not need grand settings. I have had mine watching movies, or while sitting on a rock on the top of a mountain observing the play of lights in the sky. They have come to me on a cold, wintry morning as I sipped my coffee on the balcony at home and felt the warm rays of the sun on my face, or when I have received an unexpected gift, one that I had forgotten I ever desired. And these eternal moments are also experienced through losses and pain.

My sister's recovery was, in many ways, the beginning of mine as well. The years that followed between the summer of

1996 and 2000 were my years of transition. It was a long battle through hazy and dark destinations, but His light kept guiding me out and into freedom. I had been dismantled that stormy night when I had called out to Him, and now something new was being created. It was not just a renewal process, but He was making all things new. The crucial teenage years were back, in a spiritual sense. I could not assert myself; I was at the mercy of a profound change.

Nothing had changed in the real world around me. I was back in the familiar routine of an average working girl in the city of Mumbai. But I began reacting differently to my conditions. My responses changed, and I often found myself imprisoned and isolated not just by others but by the person I had come to identify as myself in the past. I could not relate with the new thoughts and desires that sprang up from the bed of my heart each morning.

Each day had its portion of unlearning and it hurt. It hurts to give up the familiar and embrace new ways that you have never experienced before. Sometimes the bubbles of being on the threshold of a new life were submerged with the realities of office politics and daily burdens, so rapidly that it knocked me down and disheartened me.

Home had metamorphosed itself into a cold desert. I couldn't relate to the things of the past; nonetheless, I was not deserted. The Bible guided me. As I worked through its pages, I encountered God once again. The Psalms lifted me, and He taught me to pray through them. His famous Sermon on the Mount gave me hope and courage to follow the road less traveled.

Jesus said:
"Blessed are the poor in spirit,
for theirs is the kingdom of heaven.

Blessed are those who mourn,
for they will be comforted.

❖ ❖ ❖

✤ ✤ ✤

Blessed are the meek,
for they will inherit the earth.

Blessed are those who hunger and thirst for righteousness,
for they will be filled.

Blessed are the merciful,
for they will be shown mercy.

Blessed are the pure in heart,
for they will see God.

Blessed are the peacemakers,
for they will be called children of God.

Blessed are those who are persecuted because of righteousness,
for theirs is the kingdom of heaven.

Blessed are you when people insult you, persecute you and falsely say
all kinds of evil against you because of me. Rejoice and be glad, because
great is your reward in heaven, for in the same way they persecuted the
prophets who were before you."

Matthew 5:3–12

God's Word became the lamp for my feet, and He waded
with me through my troubled waters.

DA DI DA DUM DI HOLIDAY!

Here I was now, in the midst of these simple, loving folk in a beautiful house in London. The Spirit of love and warmth that engulfed me as I sat in the midst of Janis' new friends was comforting. My very tired heart felt safe here, as if it had nestled itself in the right slot within the being of my Creator. This meeting rekindled the fire that had been lit in me many, many years ago.

The prayer meeting came to a close, and I opened my eyes to the sounds of childish mirth as Josiah's daughter, Beth, glided across the room in her fairy white dress with a tiara crown set lightly on her pretty blond head. She smiled and perched herself comfortably next to me. What is it in a child's smile that makes your heart melt and spreads a warm, radiant glow within your being? I think it is yet another call of eternity. It causes a yearning for love and innocence, for purity and joy, for a carefree life and acceptance without conditions. A yearning for freedom, freedom of the kind that a child experiences under the careful vigilance of loving and doting parents. That freedom that lets her be, fully knowing that she is taken care of.

The snacks and drinks were set out after the meeting. I felt no need to strive in any manner to fit in with this gathering. I felt just at home in the midst of people who had transcended from being strangers into people I genuinely liked and felt comfortable with. Some new friendships were ignited over the next few days during my visit.

I then moved on to south Wales where I spent my time at Swansea Bay. Swansea is yet another beautiful waterfront city with magnificent views of the bay lined up with amazing eateries and bistros. But rural Swansea captured my heart with its beautiful landscapes and the ruins of Penlle'r Castell located on the highest point at Swansea. It had been a da di da dum di holiday!

I met my future husband on the stopover in Vienna, on my way back home. We got married a year later in 2003.

LAND DER BERGE

I felt like I had been living in a fairy tale during those seven days in London. I had been engrossed and woven into a tiny world of families who spent a lot of time together growing, evolving, living, and having fun. It was an ideal world. A year later I married a man whom I have come to love, adore, and treat as a part of myself. His Austrian descent brought me to the beautiful country of Austria, where I now live.

The first years in Austria came packed with all kinds of thrill rides that come along as you take in the newness of a place, its culture, and its people. It was a huge emotional roller coaster, which took its toll on me. The ups and downs and the turns and twirls of fitting into a new world brought one of my many weaknesses to the forefront. I have never considered patience to be one of my virtues, and it was what I really needed during those settling-in years. I am deeply thankful to my husband who suffered the consequences of my outbursts and tantrums and taught me patience.

The beautiful country of Austria is richly blessed with ethereal beauty. It is the land of imposing castles and cathedrals with a spectacular backdrop of majestic mountains, silver streams, and rivers merging into lush, green fields and fairy tale forests. It has risen from the ashes of two world wars and has once again become a land of hope, peace, and harmony.

I have come to appreciate and love this country immensely. The scenic villages spread on Alpine mountains, the beautiful cows from the Pinzgauer region with their unique chestnut brown sides and white underbellies, grazing on rich, green pasture lands on a late summer afternoon. Daisies, pansies, sunflowers, and poppy fields sit under the deep blue skies that reflect puffy, white, cottony clouds onto the turquoise waters of its many lakes and rivers. Lonely castles stand tall and handsome on hillocks. Yes, Austria is graceful and stunning in summer.

Autumn spreads its own shade of beauty over this blessed country, spreading its fiery yellow and orange colors over the mountains and forests, giving it a molten honey hue. This warms my heart, even as the cold wind blows and gently colors my nose a blushing red, making me aware that winter is at my doorstep.

The scene outside my window on a cold, wintry day reminds me of the land of Narnia. It is a white world. The trees are dressed in layers of white, the ground a glittering, dazzling white, and as you walk on freshly fallen snow, your heart leaps with joy when your foot sinks into the soft, powdery ground. And when the sun shines on one such wintry morning, this beautiful Narnia world comes alive—a snow white world against a deep blue sky is indeed a call from eternity.

CHANGE OF SEASONS

I grew up in the city of Mumbai, a city which houses nearly 20 million people.[3] Vienna, in sharp contrast, may reach the 2 million mark in the year 2029.[4] Mumbai can hardly be described as the land of seasons. It has mostly summer temperatures and a good four months of monsoon. My apartment in Mumbai is a tiny little five-star spot that's around fifty square meters. I love it. This is *my space*. It's an oasis of peace and beauty in the midst of a bustling city. I moved in there in 1998 and have been in and out of it ever since. Like me, it too keeps changing with time, capturing my own transitions and moods. Where in the world can I have a view of coconut trees and parrots, fighter jet eagles swooping and attacking pigeons, and crows building their nests with ingenuity that would make an architect blush? And what's more, it has the sea as its threshold, which sends in deep scents of dried fish every now and then, reminding you of its vast presence not so far away. My home in Vienna is certainly large in contrast, and I love spending a lot of time in open forests lying on endless green carpets of grass, soaking in the flavors of spring and summer, but there in those fifty square meters, my heart feels totally unrestricted.

The years between 2002 and 2005 were a phase of dramatic changes. I met my husband at the end of my UK visit in 2002, we got married within a year, and I moved to Vienna a couple of weeks after the marriage ceremony. Those three years brought about a lot of travel between Mumbai, Vienna, and London. Three years of leaving and cleaving. Three years of being swirled around in a big mixer. It wasn't just a physical relocation. I felt like God was working on me, molding me, and changing me. The changes were faster than the seasons, and I mostly felt overwhelmed with the emotional twisters.

---

[3] World Popluation Review, "Mumbai population 2014," accessed December 30, 2014, http://worldpopulationreview.com/world-cities/mumbai-population/

[4] Wien.at, population of Vienna, accessed December 30, 2014, https://www.wien.gv.at/english/living-working/population-statistics-2014.html

The scents of blooming bouquets of wildflowers on the green, mossy spring beds of earth in Vienna, mixed with the deep scents of dried fish and childhood in Mumbai, made London my neutral ground, and I strangely felt at home in London during this transition.

ALL THINGS COME TOGETHER FOR GOOD

Vienna receives very little sunshine in the months of January and February, and I tend to regularly struggle with it. It was a gray, wintry February morning, and I was at my desk near the window in our erstwhile home in Vienna, feeling rather nostalgic. That little window had become my main source of natural light during the gray, wintry days. I had taken sunlight for granted. Back at home in Mumbai, sunshine greeted me each morning, and its warm caress woke me up. But it was February and I was now in Vienna. The weather forecast had predicted a heavy-laden sky and rain showers. It would be a gray day, and I had nothing worthwhile to do. It had only been a few weeks since my move to Vienna, and my German classes were to begin in April, a good three months away. I had no one to communicate with for over ten hours in a day until my husband got home from work in the evening. A communication famine had hit upon me in a manner that I had never experienced before. I now lived in a German-speaking world and since I had not yet acquired the language, I felt very disconnected with it.

My computer seemed to be having a tough time adjusting to its new environment as well. The silence in the room was all pervasive. I felt it invading my inner sanctuary and a part of me did not want to think, feel, or acknowledge that I was at sea with no island in sight for miles. No friends, no job to go to each morning, no common language to strike up a conversation with a stranger or even explore a supermarket and examine its offerings on the shelves; everything in the supermarket was labeled in German! The sheer physical isolation from familiar neighborhoods and the absence of a daily routine was crushing.

I spent a lot of time on my computer. It was my gateway into all things familiar. As I browsed on the Internet, my mind drifted to those lovely da di da dum di days in London. To my surprise, I found a book written by Josiah on the life of the prophet Elijah; it was a free download. I began reading it. Josiah's writing facilitated a deep and introspective conversation with God that lasted for over a year. I had all the time in the world, after all, and now I had divine company.

One of the Bible verses quoted in his book has become the testimony of my life.

"And we know that in all things God works for the good of those who love him, who have been called according to his purpose."

Romans 8:28

These words of the apostle Paul, in his letter to the Romans around AD 57, released me into believing that the God Whom I had often tried to run away from had been knitting the threads of my life into a beautiful design. It was radical. How could it be true? How could He have used all the tragedies, the fears, the lies, the tears, the failures, and the heartbreaks for my good?

LUMBERING ON: EMBRACING AND LETTING GO

I thought that I had moved out of the desert. I thought that I had made peace with my Creator and genuinely believed that I could look ahead; the past was behind me, forgiven. I had no plan, only a handful of dreams and desires, which I had shared with God.

I wanted to move on but I could not. I felt grounded, stuck. And the past seemed to be catching up with me. Only this time, I knew God was in this with me. I chose to believe what I could not see. I decided to visit those dark places, the milestones of tragedy and successes, to let God show me things from my past that I had not seen from His divine perspective. I felt the shame and the humiliation of things that I had not done right, but more than that, I saw how despite my sinfulness God had given me so many chances. I could now see how He had actually come through in every situation. He had been patiently waiting for this prodigal daughter to return home. The door had been left open so His light could stream through into the darkness of my life. What I had counted as losses were actually gains now, for without those losses, I would never have come to the throne and met a God Who lives and Who seeks an intimate relationship with me.

So we lumbered together through my past, and I came to the point where I could embrace it without clinging to it. I could embrace it because God had embraced me in totality. He loved me. He had loved me, when loved ones had not. He had forgiven me, when friends had not. He was my Knight in shining armor, but unlike fairy tales, He didn't swoop me out of distress, although He could have. Instead He chose to meet me through my distress. He got off His horse and trudged along with me through my failures and shortcomings, never letting me fall beyond my own capacity to bear the consequences.

He brought me to a new place; He gave me a new home, new friends, new challenges, and adventures stood before me. Through my circumstances, He renewed me. It has been a long journey since that day at the window in February 2003. As long as we live, we will have a past. We need to deal with it in a way that does not stall our growth, but rather ignites and propels us in the right direction. Friends and fellow travelers are gemstones that God sends our way, to help us and to walk a mile or two together with us. Our stories interlink. We impact each other's lives, and we need to be conscious of it.

Josiah has been one such gemstone that God used to ignite me to walk through the closed pages of my past, to come to terms with it and to be reminded that I am loved and cherished by none other than my Creator. We all are. Our blemishes are inclusions. They make us unique. We need not reject our past. There is a God Who came down to earth and became Man to pay the price for our sins. His name is Jesus Christ. He loves us unconditionally with our blemishes. He renews us. He uses those very things that stopped us, that derailed us and limited us. He uses it all to His glory. We need to let Him in. He will search you, find you, and restore you. He is love.

YOU MET ME

You met me that night at the bus stop;
my toes were frosty, my life was a knot.
You carried me home and calmed all my fears,
You whispered shalom and wiped all my tears.

You met me that noon at the shopping mall
where she abused me, made me feel so small.
You reminded me You're my Creator.
You've woven my skin and given it color.

You met me that morning in the sunny room,
me sitting on the couch with coffee and doom.
I did not know what tomorrow would bring,
a surgery, a rift, I was driven to the brink.

You met me at the chemist, words of love You spoke,
as Grandma stretched her hand asking for a smoke.
She got no cigarette, a smile and hug instead.
Up the hill she went with flowers in her head.

Oh, how can I forget, the huge eagle You sent?
Perched on a pipe, he watched over our event.
You still my restless heart, oh how much You care.
You meet me all the time; You are always there!

This is for You, Jesus!

GOD'S LANDSCAPES

Our lives are God's landscapes. He cleans, plants, nourishes, alters the contours, and turns our souls into eternal landscapes. The Bible asserts that God is personal and God is love. The biblical narrations tell us about intimate relationships that God has had with His people right through the ages, and Jesus has made it possible for us to step into an intimate relationship with God today. God is not an abstract force. He is alive and existing, and He is directly involved in our lives here on the planet. In Jesus, I have experienced the humanness of God through my circumstances. He has cared for me and loved me, like a father does his child. I have called out to Him as a person, and His involvement in my life has been very real. It's not what I feel, but it is what He has done. He has left indelible marks of His kindness and goodness, of His discipline and justice, of His protection and wisdom, on my landscape.

"Therefore I tell you, do not worry about your life, what you will eat or drink; or about your body, what you will wear. Is not life more than food and the body more than clothes? Look at the birds of the air; they do not sow or reap or store away in barns, and yet your heavenly Father feeds them. Are you not much more valuable than they?"

Matthew 6:25–26

This is one of the most personal messages that I have ever received in my life. These words are not from some abstract force but from a heavenly Father Who cares about His creation. In these words, I find the cry of a loving God, a God Who yearns to seek us and protect us, a God Who wants us to make much more of our lives than we can possibly imagine. That is being personal. Here is a God Who empathizes. He knows about our worries, our day-to-day struggles. He knows because He is omniscient. But what makes this God so human is that He feels, He hurts with us, and He gathers our tears in the palms of His hands because He has been in such situations Himself.

He became Man, lived on this planet, and went through every possible ordeal and suffering that you could think of.

He talks solutions right into our problems. He does not expect us to ignore them, but He walks with us and pulls us out of our quicksand, just when we are sinking. He steadies us and pats us, inspiring us to move on!

AN ETERNAL LANDSCAPE

You knit me together; You gave me Your breath.
Your wounds healed me, gave my life depth.
A wonderful landscape You have drawn for me;
four decades done and there is all of eternity.

Colorful raincoats, books, and pencils,
partners for pranks, prawn curry, and pickles.
Girlhood tears, pains, and fears,
the first taste of losses, the jibes and sneers.

Ugly hearts masked as faces of love,
tossed and bruised, a wingless dove.
Death shattered my world, too early I pled!
But I had to stand up and make my own bed.

Office days full of people and meetings,
long working hours, years of seasoning.
Exotic lands and culinary delights,
amazing cultures, jet lag, and flights.

The deep blue sky from an airplane window,
the puffy, white clouds and the sunset glow.
Friends across continents, enriching encounters,
a soul mate to grow old with, in a cottage with flowers.

Thorns and roses are bunched together,
joy and pain too, are life's enrichers.
Seeking in and out, it left me depleted.
Then I chose to follow, in Him I abided.

❖ ❖ ❖

✻ ✻ ✻

"Come to Me," He said, "you who are heavy laden.
Take My yoke instead and give Me your burden.
All power in heaven and on earth lies with Me,
I'm humble and gentle at heart, you will see.
Learn from Me; let Me be your teacher.
I will hold your hand; we will walk together."

I'm glad I chose Jesus to walk through my landscape;
He chalks out the paths, my life He reshapes.
My hair is turning silver, I am going through changes,
some astounding and some bring bruises.

It's a struggle at times, my tent gives way;
just a bit of wind, can blow me away!
But He is always in time, He rebukes the storm.
He says, "Peace! Be still!" and the threat is gone.

There is so much in store, I have a lot to explore;
it is not over yet, I am ready for more.
The blessings we receive need to flow out to others.
It can't stop with us; we are God's transponders.

Thank You, Lord, You are my Creator;
my Savior, my Master, I am Your daughter.
What a privilege to know that to You I will go;
as I leave this planet, You'll be waiting at the door!

PERSONAL GOD, PERSONAL ENCOUNTERS

The stories of Abraham, Moses, and David stir an innate desire in me to keep on seeking this personal God, to have more encounters with Him, to walk in His ways, and to simply follow Him. Their walk with God was intimate and authentic.

God chose three laymen from three different ages, and He teamed up with them. He chose to renew, re-create, and revive the lives of many generations through these three men. As you read their stories in the Bible, you will note that God initiates the relationship with each one of them. He addressed them by their names, personally. He called them, talked to them, and made them a part of His plan for mankind. They doubted, protested, feared, and made mistakes but God did not give up on them. He pursued them, calmed them, and proved His intentions to them.

The encounters each one of these men had with God brings out His very own personality. He dealt with each one of them differently. He took into consideration their strengths and weaknesses, forgave their worst, and brought out the best in them. God made Abraham the father of all nations. Moses became a valiant rescuer; God used him to rescue the enslaved Israelites from the Egyptians. David, a young shepherd, was anointed as king over Israel. God called David a man after his own heart. God was personal with them. He did not order them varied tasks and leave them alone. He involved them in His plans where they played mighty roles that changed the history of mankind forever. They were His voice, His hands, and His feet.

Abraham was seventy-five years old when he had a personal encounter with God. He obeyed God's command to leave Haran with his relatives and go to the land that God would show him. Abraham journeyed by stages through the Negev as God directed him. As you read his story in the book of Genesis, you will see how God continually blessed him.

Abraham was rich but childless. Abraham and his wife, Sarah, were around ninety years old when God spoke with him in a vision.

"Do not be afraid, Abram. I am your shield, your very great reward." But Abram said, "Sovereign Lord, what can you give me since I remain childless and the one who will inherit my estate is Eliezer of Damascus?" And Abram said, "You have given me no children; so a servant in my household will be my heir."

Then the word of the Lord came to him: "This man will not be your heir, but a son who is your own flesh and blood will be your heir." He took him outside and said, "Look up at the sky and count the stars — if indeed you can count them." Then he said to him, "So shall your offspring be."

Genesis 15:1–5

It was around 2000 BC when this beautiful story of Abraham's encounters with God began unfolding. God was true to His promises. Isaac was born to Abraham's wife, Sarah, when she was way past the age of child bearing.

Exodus chapter 4 exposes the very nature of God. Here we see an almighty Father talking to His son, motivating him, egging him on, pushing him, suffering his disbelief and insecurities, and leading him on to rescue a nation. God had chosen Moses to lead and rescue the Israelites, who were enslaved by the Egyptian pharaoh, and bring them to the Promise Land. Moses hesitated; he did not want to go. Here is what ensues then between him and God:

Moses said to the Lord, "Pardon your servant, Lord. I have never been eloquent, neither in the past nor since you have spoken to your servant. I am slow of speech and tongue." The Lord said to him, "Who gave human beings their mouths? Who makes them deaf or mute? Who gives them sight or makes them blind? Is it not I, the Lord? Now go; I will help you speak and will teach you what to say." But Moses said, "Pardon your servant, Lord. Please send someone else." Then the Lord's anger burned against Moses and he said, "What about your brother, Aaron the

Levite? I know he can speak well. He is already on his way
to meet you, and he will be glad to see you. You shall speak
to him and put words in his mouth; I will help both of you
speak and will teach you what to do. He will speak to the
people for you, and it will be as if he were your mouth and
as if you were God to him. But take this staff in your hand
so you can perform the signs with it."

Exodus 4:10–17

God knows our weaknesses, and He challenges us to trust Him and let Him be the wind under our wings. Moses, indeed, led Israel out of Egypt and had many personal encounters with God over the years.

The life of David is narrated in the book of 1 Samuel and 2 Samuel. We also meet him in the book of 1 Kings, 1 Chronicles, and Psalms. The story of a young shepherd boy and his relationship with the Creator of the universe is drawn out here in all its splendor. David had a passionate relationship with God and was called a man after God's own heart; a young shepherd whom God chose to become the king of Israel. He was a gifted musician, as well, and composed some of the most compelling songs and poetry that were captured in the book of Psalms. David was a warrior under whose banner many victories were won.

He epitomizes all the highs and lows of the human species. The capability of the human race to be utterly loyal on the one hand and to be altogether despicable on the other is wonderfully gathered in these books.

The Psalms of David are some of the most intimate letters I have read from one person to another. The language is passionate and compelling. It is open, honest, trusting, seeking, and believing, even demanding at times. This is the language of love, and it clearly defines the relationship that David had with God. He had a passionate relationship with God. It was intense and active. God was His rock, His all in all.

David cries out to the Lord from the innermost depths of his being. His intimate vocabulary is witness to his intimate relationship with God. Here are a few of my favorite verses from the Psalms:

I cry aloud to the Lord; I lift up my voice to the Lord for mercy.
I pour out before him my complaint; before him I tell my trouble.
When my spirit grows faint within me, it is you who watch over my way.
In the path where I walk, people have hidden a snare for me.
Look and see, there is no one at my right hand; no one is concerned for me.
I have no refuge; no one cares for my life.
I cry to you, Lord; I say, "You are my refuge,
my portion in the land of the living."
Listen to my cry, for I am in desperate need;
rescue me from those who pursue me, for they are too strong for me.

Psalm 142:1–6

Psalm 13 gives us an insight into David's childlike heart as he pleads with his heavenly Father. He demands attention from his heavenly Father, fully trusting His ability to provide for his needs.

How long, Lord? Will you forget me forever? How long will you hide your
face from me? How long must I wrestle with my thoughts and day after
day have sorrow in my heart? How long will my enemy triumph over
me? Look on me and answer, Lord my God. Give light to my eyes,
or I will sleep in death.

Psalm 13:1–3

In Psalm 27, we see that even as David is engulfed in war, he is even more engrossed in his desire to stay close to God.

Though an army besiege me, my heart will not fear; though war break
out against me, even then I will be confident.
One thing I ask from the Lord, this only do I seek: that I may dwell in
the house of the Lord all the days of my life, to gaze on the beauty of the
Lord and to seek Him in His temple.

Psalm 27:3–4

In Psalm 104, David acknowledges God as the Creator. God's creation is personal, and He cares about each one individually.

He makes springs pour water into the ravines;
it flows between the mountains.
They give water to all the beasts of the field;
the wild donkeys quench their thirst.
The birds of the sky nest by the waters;
They sing among the branches.

He made the moon to mark the seasons;
and the sun knows when to go down.
You bring darkness it becomes night,
and all the beasts of the forests prowl.
The lions roar for their prey and seek their food from God.

Psalm 104:10–12, 19–21

CONFLUENCE

The Bible unfolds many engaging stories of ordinary men and women, over generations, interwoven into God's own story. They had a role to play, and it impacted God's story for mankind.

Over the ages, God sought ordinary folk and gave them the privilege of being a part of His story, of playing a unique role. And the story is not over yet. There is a role for each one of us to play, and it's an important one. It can influence the end. God invites us to be a part of His landscape. He designs our landscape in a manner in which it can fit into His big picture. And that big picture is eternity. It is about spending an eternity together with Him.

As we play our unique roles in this world, we converge and become parts of each other's story. There is a give and take, a confluence and a smelting, and through all of this our landscape evolves for better or worse, depending on the choices we make.

Our roles and calling cannot be quantified. You may be a mid-level employee or a secretary, a managing director or a store keeper, a doctor or an engineer, a student or a housewife. These jobs help us earn our living but, more importantly, they also provide us with a territory where we can play out our roles to the fullest.

Our stories are never ours alone. We are communicative creatures. We have the power to influence, encourage, and inspire others.

YOU ARE UNIQUE;
YOUR CALLING IS UNIQUE

Josiah has been a Bible teacher and a faithful elder, nurturing his small community in Epping, for over thirty years now. He has been serving people on other continents too, together with his wife, Mary, and daughter, Beth. Here is yet another ordinary man with an extraordinary story. He heard the Call on a normal day one summer. A normal average day turns into the most significant one in your life when you find yourself in a personal encounter with God. It may not happen as in the days of Abraham, Moses, and David, but it does happen, especially when you find yourself finally listening. That moment—when the still, calm voice of God overpowers your biggest ambitions, when you feel the gentle prodding of God's call in your chest as you relentlessly continue doing what is expected of you, or that quiet moment on a holiday when you sensed the wild calling, urging you to discover, to hunt, to seek, and to look beyond creation to the Creator.

> *Yep, inside each and every one of us is one true, authentic swing. Something we was born with, something that's ours and ours alone. Something can't be taught to you or learned. Something that got to be remembered. Over time, the world can rob us of that swing and get buried inside us under . . .all our woulda's and coulda's, and shoulda's.*
>
> Film: *The Legend of Bagger Vance*

Those are your Calls. They are invitations that God is sending out to you to meet Him; they are yours and yours alone. Those Calls, if answered, will change your life and the lives of people you encounter in a dramatic way! The beauty, romance, and suspense awaiting you are much beyond any fairy tale you have read or blockbuster movie you have seen repeatedly. When God calls you, it is a privilege and a surprise. His voice is gentle. It's a light knock on the door of your heart, but if you open that door, you get to play the role you were made for. Most of us may not be called to be Mother Teresa. We don't have to be world players. It's about doing simple things that bring about big changes on your street, in your classroom, on the playground, in the kitchen, at the restaurant, in the trains, trams, buses, taxis, at the barber shop, grocery store, work, or in the park—your story can unfold anywhere. There are things to do. You are needed. You can be the instrument God chooses to reach out to another, and you will be surprised at the people God brings your way. In so doing you have an opportunity to watch God Himself at work!

JOSIAH'S STORY

Josiah still lives with his family in London and serves his fellowship through pastoring, mentoring, and Bible teaching. Josiah has been an inspiration through his writings and teachings. The simplicities of his living and his passion to follow and be obedient to God are infectious. He has shown me by example that even in suffering we can be strong for others, not by pretending that nothing of consequence is happening to you or by putting on a bold front and claiming to be resilient, but by revealing your brokenness, by showing your vulnerability, and by crying out and pointing to the God of the cross Who saves!

Josiah used to tour with a street theater group in the UK in the early seventies. He was in his early twenties then. Outdoor work at that time in the UK got much less critical attention, and it was often audiences rather than theater critics who were more engaged with the shows and drew comparisons of street performances from year to year. So it wasn't a glamorous thing to do. You needed to have a real passion for this form of theater to be able to pursue it and adapt to its gypsy way of life. The audiences could be quite capricious. If people didn't like your show, they would just walk on. Their reactions would be completely honest, and on the streets they came from all ages and backgrounds. However, this sociopolitical setting helped drive home social and cultural messages, and Josiah felt very inclined to be a part of this world.

In the summer of 1971, Josiah and his group of performers were booked into a campsite in Cornwall. Cornwall is a peninsula that almost falls headlong into the Atlantic Ocean. This histrionic coastline has some of the most spellbinding fishing harbors and beaches. Watching the sea change colors on a sunny afternoon makes you want to take a dive and discover its turquoise bed. The smell of fish in the air around the coastline, where tall ships and boats bounce on the surface of the blue-green waters to the rhythm of the Cornish breeze, grips you into tranquility and sets you free from the chains of your to-do lists. It is a place where you must pause.

The campsite at Cornwall was close to a quaint fishing village with its fish quay, beach, and cafés, offering lovely butter scones and delicious creamy teas. Josiah loved walking through the quay and then exploring the cliff paths during his free time. They weren't the only ones on the campsite that summer. A Christian conference center had also chosen this venue for its program at the same time.

A young lad named Robert, around Josiah's age, bumped into Josiah on one of his wanderings through the cliff paths at Cornwall. He greeted Josiah and they began chatting, as most travelers do. There is something special about traveling that opens up the most discreet and reserved of us to venture and step into a chat. After all, the chances of us bumping into these fellow travelers later on are rather rare.

A quick friendship of sorts developed between Josiah and Robert as they kept bumping into each other. Sometimes it would just be a cordial nod of the head and a "Hi there," and sometimes a few words were exchanged. One evening, Robert invited Josiah and his troop to attend his conference; Josiah accepted.

JESUS LOVES YOU

Josiah's theater shows were scheduled during the day, so that let him and his friends attend the Christian conference in the evenings. His walk through cliff paths inevitably took a different turn each evening, and he found himself on the way to the conference. There were different speakers each day, and they spoke on different matters that were all connected to the Christian way of life. One evening, Josiah went to bed at the campsite very contemplative. He felt these matters of the Christian faith that were being talked about at the conference were somehow directly connected to him. They were matters of his own heart, those matters that he found difficult to articulate and talk about.

Josiah's teenage years had been full of experimental voyages of the kind that finally took him deep into the world of occultism. The mysteries of what lies beyond had always fascinated him. But all those experimental voyages had not dealt with his heart. This was new. Josiah couldn't explain the rush of tears that caught at his throat as he sat in the conference, listening to the talks. Something seemed to be happening in his otherwise stable world, something that Josiah could not fathom or control. He wished these feelings would go away; he did not want to have to articulate them. He was a street actor; he knew how to stick to a script that someone else had written. But there were new lines being written in his heart now, and he did not know how to process it. This was not a script for an actor, after all.

It was nine in the evening. The sun was setting and the sky lit up; a long, soft summer evening was upon Cornwall. Josiah strolled out of the conference center. He walked out onto the lawn, his head bent, lost in thought. He decided to walk down the quay to the local pub and down a few beers. Just as he crossed the curb, he felt a tap on his shoulder. He was caught unawares, as though someone had stepped right into his personal space. It was Graham. The tall, blond guy with the funny round glasses, the one who spoke at the conference that evening. Graham was the sort of guy who you instantly felt comfortable with. He seemed very unassuming and friendly. Graham invited Josiah to a café and Josiah accepted, almost instantly forgetting his plans to down a few beers. He liked Graham.

Graham shared his story with Josiah, and it turned out to be a long night. Josiah talked about himself with Graham too. He was excited. This was a new experience. He had never been able to speak about his life as openly as he did with Graham. What was it that made this man so endearing? He had never experienced such feelings with a stranger before.

The two men stepped out of the café. It was a beautiful night, so they decided to take a walk. Josiah felt like he had found a friend in Graham. There seemed to be a lot to talk about small things and big things, things that had never seemed important before they began surfacing. They reached a large plateau overlooking the Valency Valley and the huge expanse of sea. It was dark now; the gentle sea breeze brought in smells of the night sea right up the plateau. The unspoiled night sky put a breathtaking galaxy of stars on show, and the bats with their varied sonars were providing a melody that could not have been better composed to match the mood of nature that God had set that night.

A couple of hours went by in silent company on the plateau, and the men slowly began descending to the campsite. Josiah had to work the next morning. The time on the plateau seemed surreal. As they reached Josiah's camp, Graham smiled and hugged Josiah. He said, "Goodnight, Josiah. Jesus loves you!"

Josiah had been fighting through the week to resist that name. He didn't know why. That name had power in it. All through those evenings, it was this name that had drawn Josiah to the conference center. Yet, it had been difficult for Josiah to articulate his feelings. After all, he had never spoken with Jesus before. He had never prayed like he saw people do at the conference center. They had been talking to Jesus as though He were not just their God but an intimate friend.

Graham's words overwhelmed Josiah. As he narrated his story, he told me, "Graham came up to me and hugged me and said, 'Jesus loves you!' In that instance, I knew I was sinful and I needed His forgiveness, and all I wanted to do from that moment on was to follow Him."

FOLLOW HIM

Josiah heard the Call and chose to follow Jesus. He has been following Jesus for over forty years now. I have been inspired by Josiah. His passion for Christ shows in the way in which he leads his life. It shows through the simple things he does, simple but not easy. Josiah had a strong sense of calling to teach. He said, "As I got to know the Bible more and more, I understood that what it taught was very different from the Christianity I was seeing around me, and I wanted to teach that, and not just the traditional stuff."

Josiah has been working as a pastor and Bible teacher since 1976. He left his regular job and began full-time work as pastor and Bible teacher. He has never demanded a fee for his work. He travels across the United Kingdom and the United States on teaching assignments. He accepts whatever people choose to pay him, but he does not ask for it. Yet his work cannot, by any means, be classified as charity. I am not against works of charity, but that is the privilege of those who have enough to spare. Josiah doesn't have fat reserves in his bank account. He and his family depend on the Lord day to day. Teaching what it means to follow Jesus is a full-time occupation for Josiah. He chooses to walk in faith, to do each day what God shows him to do. And he is passionate about it.

But all his teachings and mentoring would not be effective if Josiah did not practice what he preaches. Like a teacher par excellence, he is an example of the teachings of Christ. Following Jesus is no easy task. It cannot happen unless you know Who Jesus is and unless you fall in love with Jesus, so much so that He becomes the only way, the only truth, the only life, and every other way becomes a compromise.

JUST FOLLOW HIM!

"Come follow Me," Jesus said, "and I will make you fishers of men."

You are the salt of the earth, the light of the world;
there is plenty to harvest, My kingdom to unfurl.

A city on the hill cannot be hidden;
your reward in heaven will not be stolen.

Enter through the narrow gate that leads to life;
destruction awaits those who choose gates that are wide.

Follow Me, and let the dead bury their own dead.
I have come so you may live without fear or dread.

You of little faith, why are you so afraid?
It will be done to you, according to your faith.

There is nothing concealed that will not be disclosed;
there is nothing hidden that will not be made known.

What I tell you in the dark, speak in the daylight.
What I whisper in your ear, proclaim! Don't be quiet.

Love your enemy; go help your brother.
Share your goods, gold, silver, or copper.

Hear My words and build your house on the rock.
Make Me your foundation; every disaster I can block.

Forgive and bless those who hurt you,
for you are forgiven, I have saved you.

Do not murder or commit adultery.
Do not steal or give false testimony.

Honor your father and your mother,
love yourself and also your neighbor.

Come to Me, you who are weary; I will give you rest.
I am humble and gentle, from Me you learn best.

Take My yoke — it is easy — and My burden is light;
you'll find rest for your soul, you'll be free from your plight.

A camel may pass through the eye of a needle;
your wealth can buy worldly things in ample.

But the kingdom of heaven is for the poor;
Jesus is the gate; He is heaven's door.

If you believe, you will receive; just ask in prayer.
He has all the authority, might, and power.

Follow Him! Follow Him! Oh, just follow Him!
Let's fish together, no fancies and whims!

There's a banquet to prepare for, a wedding feast;
the Bridegroom is waiting, let's bring in the harvest!

YOU MUST UNLEARN WHAT YOU HAVE LEARNED

For all of us who love the *Star Wars* series, you may remember the fifth episode when Luke Skywalker makes a trip to the Dagobah System in search of Yoda. Obi-Wan Kenobi, his ex-master, visits Luke Skywalker when he is stranded in a snowstorm and asks him if he would go to the Dagobah System to learn from Master Yoda, the Jedi master.

Luke sets a new course for his spacecraft and, along with his friend Artoo, he goes in search of the Dagobah System. As he reaches it, things start going very wrong, and he has a tough landing. It's misty, he is in the midst of a swamp jungle, and his ship has sunk in the mire. He gets nervous as he looks around him, and he begins doubting his mission. Somehow he gets the power going, opens up a can of food, and sits before the thermal heater. "Now all I have to do is find this Yoda," he tells Artoo. He does find Yoda, only Yoda does not look like a great warrior to him. The outward appearance deceives him. He tells Yoda that he is looking for a great warrior. Yoda answers, "Wars don't make you great."

And so the lessons of life begin. Luke Skywalker is in a hurry to be a Jedi. He believes he is ready for it. Yoda puts some perspective on the situation. He says, "Ready, are you? What know you of ready? For eight hundred years have I trained Jedi. My own counsel will I keep on who is to be trained! A Jedi must have the deepest commitment, the most serious mind." As they advance through the course, Yoda begins teaching Luke to move stones at first, and now it is time for Luke to move the sunken ship and bring it to the surface. Luke tries a couple of times and wants to give up. He loses hope and at that point Master Yoda serves him another life lesson. An interesting bit of dialogue ensues between the two of them.

> LUKE: Oh no! We'll never get it out now. (*He stamps his foot in irritation.*)
> YODA: So certain are you. Always with you it cannot be done. Hear you nothing that I say?

LUKE: *(Luke looks uncertainly at the ship.)* Master, moving stones around is one thing. This is totally different.

YODA: No! No different! Only different in your mind. You must unlearn what you have learned.

LUKE: *(Focusing uncertainly.)* All right, I'll give it a try.

YODA: No! Try not. Do. Or do not. There is no try.

Luke closes his eyes and concentrates on thinking the ship out; the X-wing's nose begins to rise above the water. It hovers for a moment and then slides back, disappearing once again.

LUKE: *(Panting heavily.)* I can't. It's too big.

YODA: Size matters not. Look at me. Judge me by my size, do you? Hmm? Hmm. And well you should not. For my ally is the Force, and a powerful ally it is. Life creates it, makes it grow. Its energy surrounds us and binds us. Luminous beings are we, not this crude matter. You must feel the Force around you, here, between you, me, the tree, the rock, everywhere, yes. Even between the land and the ship.

LUKE: *(Discouraged.)* You want the impossible.

With his eyes closed and his head bowed, Yoda raises his arm and points at the ship and the entire X-wing moves gloriously toward the shore. Luke stares in disbelief as the spacecraft settles down onto the shore.

LUKE: I don't . . . I don't believe it.

YODA: That is why you fail.

Yoda shakes his head, bewildered.
Yoda basically imparts three principles to his disciple, Luke Skywalker:

You must unlearn what you have learned.
Do not try to do something, but do it.
Belief is key.

Much of that conversation between Yoda and Luke holds true for those of us who choose to follow Jesus. In the Christian life, belief is key. What do you believe in? Where have you placed your faith? The object of our belief triggers most of our actions or inactions.

When we place our belief in Jesus, we stop living out of self-belief. That in itself is a radical shift. And once we have chosen to do so, it brings about a learning process. We find ourselves in a classroom with God as our teacher. It feels defeating at times because there is so much to unlearn. We receive a new perspective, and we begin to see the world differently.

Josiah shared what that meant for him when he decided to follow Jesus. He said, "What I saw in scripture is that following the Lord should affect every area of life and not just some. The church life stood out for me, but so did family life, and the way in which everything should be through close relationships with those around us, rather than the closed-off and selfish lives that many of us seemed to be living. Although scripture doesn't teach that it is wrong to have nice possessions, it was, nevertheless, clear to me that giving for most of us amounted to dropping crumbs under the table rather than anything actually sacrificial."

Most of us try really hard to live biblically and are frustrated. We cannot do it on our own. We need to feel the force of the one true and living God in us and around us. We need to lean on that force. We have to let go of our own negligible strength and let His strength flow through us. Then we are able to do more, much more. That is what God has promised us in His Word.

"But He said to me, 'My grace is sufficient for you, for my power is made perfect in weakness.' Therefore I will boast all the more gladly about my weaknesses, so that Christ's power may rest on me. That is why, for Christ's sake, I delight in weaknesses, in insults, in hardships, in persecutions, in difficulties. For when I am weak, then I am strong."

2 Corinthians 12:9–10

EVERY WEAKNESS
IS AN OPPORTUNITY

Josiah is undergoing chemotherapy right now as I write this. He has been through an eight-hour surgery for colon cancer and was grounded for a year. It is a privilege to be a part of his journey, to walk a bit on quicksand together with him.

Every weakness is an opportunity to let the power of Christ shine through us. As Paul said in his second letter to the Corinthians, "For when I am weak, then I am strong" (2 Corinthians 12:10).

Josiah's illness has physically grounded him, but I also see that his ability to share, teach, encourage, and mentor has been enriched through his current circumstances. He may not be able to travel physically, but with technology he has made himself accessible to others. His humor hasn't deserted him either. His sickness and recovery have encouraged and enlightened many of us because he chooses to share. He lets others see his vulnerability and utter dependence on God. He chooses to encourage us and be encouraged himself. At a critical time as this, when you are undergoing chemotherapy where day-to-day living can be challenging, you have no control over tomorrow and each day is unpredictable. It is overwhelming to see Josiah's struggles and successes, and I have learned many precious lessons through him.

Josiah lay in the intensive care ward of a hospital in London. After eight hours of surgery, his condition remained very critical for a few days. He shared with me later:

> I knew, of course, that everything hinged on me deliberately, and definitely, laying hold of the Lord and maintaining thankfulness for all, for His many blessings to me, the greatest of all being my salvation. I suppose I could have taken the route of depression and self-pity instead. But I knew that nothing in reality has changed just because the light has dimmed. The Lord has never changed, nor will

He, and He was as worthy of my praise, worship and obedience the moment I found out about the cancer as He was whilst I was blissfully unaware of it. The verse that therefore dominated my thinking throughout that week was, "Thou wilt keep him in perfect peace, whose mind is stayed on thee: because he trusteth in thee" (Isaiah 26:3, KJV).

Josiah, I salute you!

PART 5: PEARL

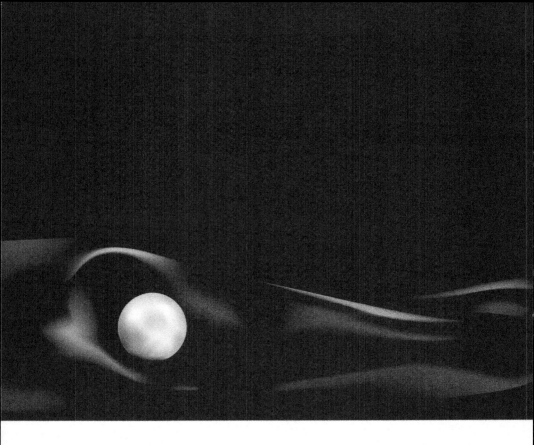

PEARL

Where do I begin with the story of Pearl?
She was a beautiful maiden, her head full of curls.
Lovely and shy, a child full of woes,
cows to milk and a lot of house chores.

The lantern burned bright in the cowshed one night,
Pearl was studying there, with the cows by her side.
She fell asleep on the hay, she was exhausted to the core;
a price she had to pay for being a maiden among boars.

The brothers got the best of the broth;
Pearl had to scrape the bottom of the pot!
Such were her beginnings, but out of the ashes she rose;
her Creator she sought, she withstood all her foes.

But her heart never changed, she didn't hold a grudge,
she was loyal and giving, she didn't judge.
Another Pearl there can never be,
this is her story, her life inspired me!

Many broken hearts she touched
with her kindness and mercy.
A pearl she was, reflecting inner beauty.
And a tough Pearl at that, full of grit and spunky.

Pearl was my mother.
She has gone home to be with the Lord.
I miss her. She is indeed my pearl!

SORROWFUL BEGINNINGS

Pearl was born on July 7, 1939 in a small town in Mangalore, a coastal city in the southwest of India. Her father was the sole bread winner of the family. In those days, most women in this little town stayed at home, looked after the family, and contributed to their husband's livelihood in whatever way they could. Pearl's mother, Sophia, was the cord that held this family of ten together. Pearl's father was a tailor by profession, but he lost all his fortunes that were stored in a wooden trunk to a fire that broke out and burned down most of the house. He counted his losses, picked up a small farm, and became a farmer. Pearl was around five years old at that time, and this riches-to-rags story dramatically affected her life. She found herself spending more time in the kitchen, helping her mother rather than playing outside in the yard with her other siblings. She was too young to understand what had happened, but the course of her life changed forever.

Her mother had a preference for male children and believed her sons to be the family heirs who would restore prosperity in the household in the future. She chose to treat her sons as investments, and the daughters were to be the tools through which she would serve these heirs and ensure that they had the best she possibly could afford. Pearl's older sisters ran off to the bigger cities as fast as they possibly could in search of careers and opportunities. But Pearl was much too young; she was the fifth child out of eight and the last of the girls. There were years when she was the only girl along with her mother, feeding and caring for four men in the family. Those were the years of Pearl's slavery. She wasn't treated like a precious daughter but made to feel like a worthless slave.

PEARL'S CHILDHOOD

Mangalore is a harbor city enclosed on the east by the Arabian Sea and on the west by the Western Ghats mountain ranges. It is a city where rivers melt into each other, waterfalls pave their way over solid rocks, and pristine beaches provide solace and rest. When I was a child, Pearl took me by train on summer holidays to her hometown. It was an overnight journey, and I remember Pearl waking me up excitedly early in the morning to catch the sunrise outside the train window. But most of all I loved the bright spots of green all along the way, farmlands that signaled that I was close to where my grandmother lived, and she was always nice to me.

Pearl's childhood centered around her father's few acres of land, her school, her home, and church. All of these places were five kilometers from one another; her boundaries were very limiting.

Pearl's day began at 4:00 a.m. She would help her mother with the morning chores, then run to school and be back in time to milk the cows. After lunch, she would help out at the farm and then aid her mother with dinner preparations. She and her mother would eat last, after all the boys were fed. On most occasions, there would not be enough food left and Pearl would have to scrape the bottom of the pot out of sheer hunger. But the day wasn't over yet. She would wash up, close the kitchen, and then carry her lamp with her to the cowshed where she finally could do what she loved doing most — studying. The cows greeted Pearl with delight each night as she stepped into the cowshed along with her books and settled on the hay in a corner. But before she began studying and tackling her homework, she would gently pat each cow by name and talk to them. They would *moo* in answer, and a conversation ensued, which only Pearl and the cows understood. Those were her sacred moments, her favorite time of the day. After a couple of hours when she was done with her school homework, she would tiptoe back into the house to the room where her mattress lay on the floor. Another day had finally come to an end. And so it went on until Pearl reached her late teens. She finished high school and headed to the city of Mumbai, where her older sisters lived.

TRANSITION

Pearl was seventeen years old when she came to the big city of Mumbai. Her older sister Alicia was married to an alcoholic. Peter would come home drunk each night and disrupt everyone's sleep with his abusive growls and aggressive gestures. Pearl received a letter from Alicia one day. Alicia was distraught and wanted to end her life; she clearly needed help. Pearl now had a choice. She had a choice to continue staying in the world she knew and keep on doing things that were familiar, or let go, move, and take the dive into an unknown world.

She moved to the big city to help Alicia. Pearl moved from a farmhouse in the village to a tiny apartment in a chawl, in the suburbs of Mumbai. Pearl went through radical experiences that charted the course of her life. She shared thirty-five square meters of space with seven people. Privacy did not exist and still does not for most people living in the slums and chawls in Mumbai.

A chawl is a large tenement found mainly in South Asia. This large tenement is divided into many apartments that are economically priced. Each floor has a set of toilets outside the apartments. The sheer congestion and close proximity of these apartments to one another prohibits private living—the main doors are mostly left open and there are comings and goings all the time. The entire building turns into one big family. They look out for each other, share their food, and participate in the lives of their neighbors.

Pearl was disoriented at first, traveling in overcrowded trains and buses, learning new languages, and hunting for a job. Alicia went to work early in the morning and came home late in the evening. She leaned heavily on Pearl, and she would mostly come home sobbing and narrating her ongoing battles with her husband, Peter.

Pearl missed her cowshed; she missed her cows.

YOUNG, SINGLE BUT NEVER FREE

It was a hot and humid summer night. People in Mumbai had been praying desperately to their varied gods and goddesses, seeking much-needed respite from the heat; after all, monsoons were almost on Mumbai's doorstep, and they would bring relief.

Pearl found it hard to sleep. She had as much space as in a tiny sleeping bag, and the children were sprawled all over the floor next to her. Suddenly, a cool breeze made its way through the open window. Pearl looked upward at the window and saw the willowy crescent of the moon. She took in a deep breath and quietly stood up. She decided to step out for a walk. Making her way carefully through the sleeping bodies sprawled on the floor, Pearl slipped on her sandals, which she always left outside the door, and made her way to the stairway. As she stepped out of the building, the fresh scent of jasmines greeted her; they grew in abundance in the tiny patch of garden toward the left wing of the building. She made her way to the garden, as if being magically drawn by the scent of those flowers.

Pearl took in deep breaths and strolling along the pathway between shrubs and bushes she reached an old wooden bench that creaked when she sat on it. It was a strong, wooden bench though and had seen many seasons in this park; many had signed their names on it for posterity. Pearl glanced up at the sky and began praying. It had been a year since she moved to Mumbai, and it had been a turbulent year at that. But today had been a special day. She had found herself a job as an accountant in a government organization because of her mathematical skills. Her future boss had been surprised by her excellent grades. He asked her why she had stopped studying. "Pearl, you have a lot of potential. You are only eighteen. Are you sure you want to start work?" Pearl nodded in affirmation.

Pearl looked up once again at the dark, starry sky and thanked God for the blessing she had received that day. The tears began to pour, even in her state of thankfulness. She had tried hard to be positive about this big opportunity that had come her way, but she would have given anything to be able to study further! She loved mathematics and the sciences. Oh, how she loved those subjects! Her school teacher, Mrs. Karkara, had pleaded with her parents to let her study further. They had offered to waive the fees for the first few semesters, but Sophia could not make any sense of her daughter's desires to study further. She had already allowed it to go on for too long.

As Pearl sat on the wooden bench praying, memories of the past kept stepping in, inflicting pain. Hot tears of frustration poured down her cheeks as she asked God, "Why, Lord why? Why couldn't I study further? But now that You have given me a job, I will use it to educate myself, to serve others, and to help my poor family; after all, my nephew and nieces need me. With Your help, I will go on. Please help me to forgive my parents and guide my path ahead. I need you!" She resolved to move on, to embrace the future, and to take on the challenges. She would devote her life to those who needed love and care. She chose to give those very things that she had most yearned for, those things that she had not received. One of Pearl's favorite prayers was from St. Francis of Assisi.[5]

Lord, make me an instrument of your peace;
Where there is hatred, let me sow love;
Where there is injury, pardon;
Where there is discord, harmony;
Where there is error, truth;
Where there is doubt, faith;
Where there is despair, hope
Where there is darkness, light;
And where there is sadness, joy.
O Divine Master,
Grant that I may not so much seek, to be consoled as to console;
To be understood, as to understand;
To be loved, as to love;
For it is in giving that we receive,
It is in pardoning that we are pardoned,
And it is in dying that we are born to Eternal Life.

---

[5] "The Prayer of Saint Francis," Christian prayer first printed in a French magazine in 1912, accessed 12/3/14, http://en.wikipedia.org/wiki/Prayer_of_Saint_Francis. Public domain.

Pearl chose to spend the rest of her life comforting, consoling, loving, and giving. She chose to believe that these noble things are worth living for, and kindness and mercy are planted in the hearts of those who choose to follow God. She chose to give her time to others, never free for herself but always available to those in need.

A DECADE OF STRUGGLE

Pearl swung back and forth between her career and Alicia's kids over the next ten years. She ensured that all four of them were well grounded in their education. They were sent to private schools as Pearl generously contributed most of her income to run Alicia's household. The children grew attached to Pearl, and they felt secure knowing that she was accessible to them. Pearl received regular promotions at work, and after a decade she became the team leader of a small group of accountants. The team adored her. Pearl was their mentor and guide. She took the time to get to know each one personally. She was deeply interested in understanding their needs, their personal challenges, their goals, and long-term objectives. Their goals were her goals; their challenges were hers as well.

Pearl carried the same values she practiced at home to the workplace. She was compassionate, caring, and giving. "Pearl Madam was so careful about her work. She was so good with numbers, and she always covered up for our deficiency," said Betty one afternoon. Chandra's eyes welled up with tears at the thought of Pearl. "She was like a mother to me. She taught me my job. When I was ill or had to go home early for personal reasons, she would do my work, if it could not wait for tomorrow. She was so loving and generous with her time and skills." Most of Pearl's close colleagues remember her as a loving teacher who taught them the lessons of life. A loving teacher, who set high moral standards and did not compromise on her values.

Pearl defined these years as years of struggle for herself. She put her back into everything she did. She endeavored to be a mother to her sister's kids, to be a mentor and trainer to her team at work, to be a friendly neighbor who people called on often for help and sometimes just for a motivational chat, and to be a serving daughter and meet the demands made by her long-distance parents. It was a struggle, one that she willingly accepted. She chose to live for others. She wasn't blind to the influence of money, and she had become aware of the power of her womanhood as well. Pearl was a dainty, pale-skinned woman with dark hair and a melancholy smile. Men were drawn to her, indeed, but Pearl chose to ignore it all. She stayed focused on her goals.

Her struggle had a purpose; she knew she had been called to help rebuild a broken home of six. Her sister Alicia had been deeply wounded with the disappointments in her marriage and the physical abuse that she had been subjected to by a very drunken husband. The children had witnessed far too much for their years. They had seen and heard things that children must not be exposed to. Lenny, Natty, Winnie, and Doris were all between three and ten years old when Pearl had moved in with them.

PETER

The children were slowly growing strong and secure. They adored Pearl. She cooked delicious food, gave them gifts, helped them with their homework, and put them to bed each night with a lovely song. She sang the songs she had learned in school back in Mangalore. She had a soothing voice, and it helped dim out the pressures of the day.

It was monsoon time again. The Mumbai monsoons are famous for their nonstop pitter-patter that goes on from early June until the end of September each year. Monsoons are extremely challenging for the large middle-class population of this city that mainly travels by the railway. Some reports suggest that 7.5 million people travel by trains every single day in Mumbai, and the Mumbai Suburban Railway is the busiest rapid transit system in the world. The trains are severely overcrowded, and the railway tracks get flooded during monsoons. Some people lose their lives when they lean outside the doors and get hit by electric poles, or they sit on the roof of the trains and get electrocuted. The lack of space in the trains and the need to get to work punctually leaves very few options for the commuters. Railway accidents happen all through the year, but they peak during the monsoons.

It had been raining hard one morning, and Pearl was wondering if she could take a day off. She knew that the schools would close earlier than usual on such a rainy day, and it would be nice to spend the afternoon with the kids playing board games, sipping hot chai, and eating spicy Indian snacks, which they all loved.

It was around ten in the morning when Pearl stepped out to call her office from a public phone booth. Those were the days when average Indians couldn't afford a landline connection at home. When she came back home and took off her sandals at the doorstep, she found Peter's shoes lying there too. She stopped for a moment, fear clutching her heart. Why was he home? He had gone to work as he usually did. On most morning's, he never really reached his office and headed straight for the bar. Peter worked with the Indian railways. He never brought his salary home, and for years, he had been drinking away all the money he received.

Pearl had taken a very brave step a couple of months ago. She traveled to Peter's office on her own and met Peter's boss and colleagues. She enlightened them on Peter's domestic situation. Peter's boss was a compassionate man, and he made a decision to send Peter's salary home directly so he would not have access to it. Perhaps this had irritated Peter? Pearl whispered a prayer to the Lord and stepped in, expecting the worst.

Peter was a tall, dark man. He had slender shoulders that drooped far too early for his age. He was around forty years old but looked much older. Peter was sitting at the window on a stool. His head was buried in his hands, and Pearl could not see the expression in his eyes, but his body language suggested some sort of mental or physical ill health. Pearl kept her distance and politely asked him what the matter was. He did not respond at first. Then after a couple of moments, he turned away from the window, lifted his head, and looked at Pearl.

His dark brown eyes were clouded with tears. Pearl witnessed a calm and almost soft expression on Peter's face for the first time. What had brought this about? She asked him if he would like a cup of chai. He nodded in agreement. The kitchenette in this apartment was a tiny corner, but it served its purpose; meals for seven were cooked out of this cramped space each day. The kerosene stove was small, but it was a strong machine and had never let Pearl down. She lit the stove and put the kettle of water on it to boil. Pearl was perturbed. As she waited for the chai to brew, many thoughts crossed her mind. Had Peter lost his job? Was he ill? She quickly murmured a prayer to the Lord, asking Him to intervene and help her converse with Peter.

LOVE REFLECTS

Pearl placed the two cups of chai on the table near Peter. He picked up one of them, took a sip, and kept staring at the mug very lost in his thoughts. Pearl decided to wait patiently and not question him. She wanted him to talk. He had hardly spoken with her over the years, only what was necessary.

"I want to thank you for what you have done for me and my family, Pearl!" he blurted out in a sudden rush of words. "You are a reflection of God's love; for what else could drive you to do what you do every single day for my children, for Alicia, for me? You have been upset with me, and I know I deserve it. I have done many wrong things. I want to change. I want to stop drinking."

Peter's boss, Danish, had called Peter into his room at the office the evening before and had given him a final warning. He would lose his job if he continued coming in late and drunk. On the way home that evening, as Peter closed in on the bar that he frequented every day, sometimes many times a day, he found himself retreating and walking in a different direction. He had not allowed himself to think for years, and he had carefully hidden his soul from Memory herself, lest she should trouble and provoke him into any sort of change that he was not prepared for. He wanted life to be status quo. Alcohol had grown on him and eaten away at his very being. What had begun as a small pleasure after the hard work had soon turned into a full-blown addiction. He remembered the first time he met Alicia. It was during a Christmas party in 1949. Soon it would be the turn of a decade, and that meant a lot to Indians. India had been set free on August 15, 1947, from the British Raj. It took time for India to comprehend this great reality and to adapt to freedom. The turn of the decade symbolized a new beginning in many ways. Alicia was at that party too, and they had talked all night. They met regularly for chai at a small Iranian café in Byculla, close to Alicia's office. Those chats over chai turned into dreams of companionship, marriage, children, and happily ever after. The happily ever after lasted for a few months, before the challenges of daily life overwhelmed him, and he turned to alcohol for solace.

THE DAM BURST

Peter had been walking for quite a while after hearing the shocking news from his boss. He had reached the shore of the sea and made his way to one of the cemented seats facing the water. It was dark. The sun had set, and people were out strolling on the promenade taking digestive walks after a heavy dinner. Dinner times were sacred in this city. It was family time and everyone made it to the dinner table.

It was quite noisy on the promenade, but Peter was isolated in his thoughts. He felt like he was waking up from a deep slumber. He thought of his children, those wonderful gifts that God had given him. He loved them but caring for their needs had overwhelmed him. He felt he could not be a good father, he felt crushed by their emotional demands, and he felt he could not share that with Alicia. He thought she would not have understood him.

But a young teenage girl from the village had set an example. When Pearl had arrived in Mumbai, he thought this would be yet another mouth to feed and take care of. However, the grace with which she had generously shared her time, abilities, and her very life itself with all of them had astounded him. Her income had helped pay the school fees for four. Why was she doing it? What or who was behind this generosity without boundaries, without wanting something in return? The questions kept coming at Peter with every fresh gush of sea breeze; he began breathing hard and his heartbeats quickened, or perhaps he was listening in for the first time. The tears came, and the dam burst. Peter thought about God. The last time he had thought about God was at the Garden of Remembrance when they buried his father. He had been upset because his dad was young — and his best friend. He had never spoken with God after that day. But this evening he did. He spoke his heart out at that sea front. He pelted his words across at the deep, black expanse of sea that could not be seen in the darkness but could be heard. His tears turned into relentless, convulsive howls. Peter sat in this attitude of repentance for hours that night at the sea front. Then he asked God to forgive him.

He stood up from that cement seat — way past midnight — and for the first time in years, he made his way back home sober and anxious to meet his family. He reached home and he tried to carefully walk around, not wanting to wake anyone up, especially the kids. They looked angelic in their sleep.

The next morning, Peter set out to work, as usual, but he could not. He needed to rest. The years of indulgence had impacted his body. He felt remorse. He called his boss from a public phone and requested a day off. Danish took the request rather kindly, and Peter was relieved. He made his way back home wanting to spend some quiet time there. He wasn't expecting Pearl, as she was usually at the office. Alicia came home from work that evening and was surprised to see Peter there. Her first instincts were panic driven. She wondered if he had lost his job finally and now they would be in a real financial mess. Peter spoke with Alicia and calmed her fears, but she wasn't thrilled. Peter had promised to give up alcohol many times before, only to return to it with a lot more gusto. She found it hard to believe him.

Later that night, Alicia and Pearl strolled in the garden after dinner and settled themselves on the wooden bench. Pearl encouraged Alicia to give Peter a chance. "I am sure God is changing his heart, Alicia! I have been praying for this moment for years, and he sounded very sincere this morning. We need to forgive him. We need to give him a chance. God can restore what has been broken." Pearl lovingly placed her arm around Alicia's shoulder.

WHEN FREDDY MET HIS PEARL . . .

M y father loved narrating his story, especially about the
time when he met my mother. He once shared his story
with a dear friend who had joined us for lunch. It was one of
his most passionate and tender narrations. I have recounted it
here for you.

I was thirty-six years old, a confirmed bachelor.
That is how I defined my status at that time. But
my mother played a trick on me. She advertised in
the *Times of India*, India's largest selling newspaper
at that time. It was January 1965. I was nursing
a broken heart. I had a job with an American-
based engineering company, a handsome salary,

and company quarters to live in. My normal day would begin at around 8:00 a.m. Mother lived with me. She would serve me breakfast, and a rich south Indian breakfast at that. Hot dosas[6] with chutney and sambhar[7] or idlis;[8] actually I preferred idlis, steaming hot idlis! I could eat around a dozen or more at a time. I had a ferocious appetite, and I loved my south Indian food. The New Year had begun well, and I was due for a promotion that year. That meant a raise in salary. Things were good for me. But Mother didn't think so. My younger brother, Steve, was happily married and had four children. Mother wanted the same destiny for me. So she advertised in the *Times of India*, in the matrimonial section: "Handsome, well-to-do, Keralite boy is looking out for a beautiful, educated working girl," or something to that effect. I had no clue about it then. A month later, she showed me a specific response with a black-and-white photograph of Pearl.

I didn't think much of it all then; actually I didn't pay much attention. I thought Mother would let it pass and forget about it in a while, but she didn't. She instead sent a reply to the address from where she had received Pearl's resume and stated our interest in meeting the girl and her family! My mother was a strong-headed lady. She lost her husband when she was thirty-eight years old, and she had looked out for us since then. She was a successful woman. She took over and ensured that her kids had a secure upbringing. It was not easy;

---

[6] A dosa is a pancake made from rice flour and ground pulses. It is sometimes served with various fillings, such as potatoes or vegetables.

[7] Sambar is a vegetable stew or chowder made with lentils.

[8] Idlis are South Indian steamed cakes of rice, and they are usually served with a lentil curry and coriander chutney.

times were hard, and I respect her for what she has done. I'm proud of her.

So a meeting was set. Pearl's family invited us to her sister's place. We were warmly greeted. A lot of small talk dominated the first hour. Then Mother requested to see the girl for whom we had traveled two hours in the afternoon sun. I had actually kept the taxi waiting because I estimated this entire affair to last for a couple of minutes. I naturally would leave my answer open to interpretation and move out of there as fast as I could. That was the plan!

Pearl's older sisters hurried into an inner room; they were cajoling Pearl to step outside. We could hear loud, agitated whispers and hushed tones. And then, all of a sudden, there she was, standing before me. She was the most beautiful person I had ever encountered in my entire life! I couldn't breathe. She stood there before me, clad in a simple sari with her eyes cast down. Her older sister introduced us. I stretched out my hand. She very feebly gave hers, and our eyes met for one fleeting moment. That was all. She never looked at me after that all through the time we were there. But it didn't matter. I had fallen in love with her! I wanted to marry her, and as soon as possible . . .

LET MARRIAGE
SUSTAIN YOUR LOVE

From now on, it is not love that sustains your marriage,
but marriage that sustains your love.

Dietrich Bonhoeffer, *Letters and Papers from Prison*

Pearl married Freddy on February 16, 1966. The transition was hard for both of them. Lenny, Natty, Winnie, and Doris had a very difficult time not having Aunty Pearl around them every day. Pearl visited the children every evening after work for a long time, as long as she was needed; the cords of love kept pulling. There were comings and goings between these two households for many, many years until all the children had graduated and settled down.

Pearl and Freddy had two daughters of their own. They had wished for daughters, and that is what they received. Pearl taught her daughters to believe in dreams, to try for the best but to be content with the least.

Pearl and Freddy had an open-door policy. Neighbors, friends, colleagues, and relatives rang the bell of their home unannounced. Be it loving advice; a plate full of yummy, hot food; a listening ear; financial help; prayers; a shoulder to lean on; a bed to sleep in; or simply jovial company, people knew they would not be refused in this home.

Pearl had to count the pennies on many occasions and even though she and Freddy were both working, their salaries were meager and all of it was spent on the basics of living. But this home had the fragrance of warmth and abundance to all who came visiting. Pearl believed in a selfless culture. She said, "We weren't meant to live for ourselves. We may not achieve our dreams, but we can be the vessels through which others can fulfill theirs."

Pearl did not start a movement to change the world, but she inspired those in the circle of her influence to want to live their lives differently. She had been wounded and her self-esteem had been badly hurt as a child, but she let the light, the kindness, the joy, and the grace of God flow out through those very cracks of pain that her experiences had etched on her being.

Pearl touched individual lives through her love. She wasn't very articulate with words, which is probably why her actions spoke so loudly. She also had the gift of touch. Her soothing touch and her shy smile warmed many, many hearts.

PEARL AND SOPHIA

Pearl helped many broken hearts heal, including that of her mother. Sophia's investment in the male heirs of the family turned out to be fruitless. All of her precious sons deserted her in her old age.

It was the month of May 1978, summertime in India when temperatures rise. Pearl and Freddy were on the way to the railway station to pick up her mother, Sophia. Station Road, as it is called in Mulund, was one of the many chaotic streets in Mumbai. The long street narrowed and curved toward the entrance to the railway station where thousands of people constantly moved in and out, mostly in a desperate rush from one destination to another. It's overcrowded and it's not uncommon to feel light-headed from the close proximity to masses of sweaty human bodies, all moving together in one direction or another. Added to the chaos, the narrow street was lined with vendors on both sides, selling anything from fruits and vegetables to shoes and household goods.

It was mango season, and the air that noon was scented with delightful variations of this golden fruit. An Indian mango has golden, pulpy, sweet nectar! Indians call it the king of fruits and elatedly await its arrival each summer. People eat this fruit for breakfast, lunch, and dinner in the summer months. Mangos are bought not in dozens but in baskets of hundreds, when affordable.

The air was charged with hectic activity, each vendor outdoing the other on vocals, wooing people to their carts. People walked along at a busy pace, stopping at the vendors, bargaining and buying. Freddy held Pearl's hand and ingeniously made the way through this thick maze to the entrance of the railway station.

Pearl and Freddy were just in time to see the train pull in. Sophia had arrived from Magalore at the Victoria Terminus Station in the afternoon. The trip from the Victoria Terminus Station to the railway station at Mulund had taken another hour. But since it was afternoon, the trains were rather empty, and Sophia had sufficient space to be seated and manage her luggage. She didn't have much, just a suitcase with her personal belongings and another smaller one with goodies for Pearl's daughters.

Sophia was sixty-eight years old now. Life had not turned out the way she thought it would. She was given away in marriage at the age of sixteen. She had her first child when she was barely seventeen, and after three miscarriages, she had eight children left. She had always believed that her boys would look after her and treat her well when they grew up. But each one of them had disappointed her. Now even the youngest son had deserted her. She was not needed anymore. She had barely had enough food to eat in the last months, and melancholy had filled her very being. Sophia reached out to the one daughter who would hear her cry. Pearl responded to Sophia's call for help. She discussed the situation with Freddy, and they decided to welcome Sophia into their home and into their lives. Freddy loved Sophia as he would his own mother, and the children were excited to have Grandma living with them.

The train pulled into the station, and Pearl spotted the skinny, small frame of her mother dressed in a deep blue cotton sari with her long, thick, silver gray hair bundled up into a bun at the back of her neck. Pearl loved her mother despite everything that had transpired between them during her childhood; she ran to greet her and gave her a warm, welcoming hug. Freddy carried the suitcases, and they made their way back home once again through the busy station road.

Sophia lived with Pearl and her family until she died at the age of seventy-two. Those four years were precious for everyone concerned. She was loved by all. Pearl's daughters couldn't wait to come home from school each day. They knew Grandma would have cooked yummy things for them. Grandma was a beautiful, old lady with supple skin, and her face crinkled into layers when she smiled. Her dark eyes had softened with the years, and her hair was thick and long, even at that age. Sophia was poised and elegant. She was always clad in a sari and a long, gold chain with a cross around her neck—that was the only piece of jewelry she had managed to keep for herself.

LOVE HEALS

A deep bond developed between Pearl and Sophia over those four years when they lived together in Mumbai. They spent a lot of time with each other talking, sharing, praying, forgiving, and comforting. It did not happen in a day, but over those four years a lot of love was given and received. Sophia was mostly overwhelmed with her daughter's generosity and love. How can we offer love to those who have not given it to us? How can we love those who have repelled us and made us feel that our existence here on earth is of no consequence? The Bible says that God so loved the world that He gave His only Son for us.

"This is love: not that we loved God, but that he loved us and sent his Son as an atoning sacrifice for our sins. Dear friends, since God so loved us, we also ought to love one another. No one has ever seen God; but if we love one another, God lives in us and his love is made complete in us."

1 John 4:10–12

Pearl could give because she did indeed receive. Pearl had a deep conviction about the love of Christ. She was convinced that God loved each and every one of us. The symbol of her conviction was the cross—the cross of Christ. It was the love of Christ that had seen her through challenging situations in her childhood and throughout her entire adult life. It was the same love that had enabled her to sacrifice many years of her life to lift up a broken family. People remember Pearl as someone who always put others first. She believed in loving in spite of. And she always pointed to the source that made it possible—to Christ.

"If you love those who love you, what credit is that to you? Even sinners love those who love them. And if you do good to those who are good to you, what credit is that to you? Even sinners do that. And if you lend to those from whom

you expect repayment, what credit is that to you? Even
sinners lend to sinners, expecting to be repaid in full.
But love your enemies, do good to them, and lend to them
without expecting to get anything back. Then your reward
will be great, and you will be children of the Most High,
because he is kind to the ungrateful and wicked.
Be merciful, just as your Father is merciful."

Luke 6:32–36

Pearl died at the age of forty-nine on June 12, 1988. But love never dies. Her love impacted many lives. People remember that love and draw inspiration from it even now. Twenty-six years have gone by since anyone of us saw Pearl in person. But her kind heart and generous giving ignites a desire in us to do the same.

I RECALL

I am Pearl's daughter. I miss her. I have shared her story — her walk on quicksand — not because she was my mother, but because she was so much more to so many people. She was a mother to many of my friends, a confidential friend to many lonely travelers, and a guide and a valuable mentor to some. But in all the different roles she played, she was compassionate and loving. I had the unique privilege of being her confidante during the last years of her life. She shared her story with me, all that I could not have known or observed. She prepared me for life, for the times when she would not accompany me. She gave me many precious gifts, but the best thing she ever did was tell me the story of Jesus.

Good Fridays were special to us. The house would be extraordinarily quiet on a Good Friday. It was a day of reflection and soul searching. Her silence and full stop to the normal buzz of life on Good Friday taught me the importance of being still from time to time. She managed to have her Good Friday moments throughout the year despite her busy schedule. She also made time to dream with me.

The Easter break and its significance meant more to my mother than Christmas or any other time of the year. I remember lying on her lap one afternoon and listening to the story of Jesus, about His crucifixion. Mother had narrated that story on many Good Fridays before. It was a sort of a ritual. But she had a beautiful voice, very soothing, and when she told a story I felt secure. Story time for me was "feeling secure" time, a time of special bonding. But this one Good Friday narration was special.

I must have been around twelve years old. The tears clutched at my throat as Mom told me about the nails that were hammered into the hands of the Lord Jesus; she said that was my punishment that He had taken for me, for her, and for all of humanity. I took one of my pencils a couple of hours later and tried to stick its tip into the palm of my hand. Naturally, I did not succeed; the pain was too much. My eyes burned with tears;

I was too young to understand and appreciate such love from a God Who I had not really met then. But Mom had planted the seed in my heart.

Thank you, Mother, for this gift you gave me. Thank you for initiating me into the biggest love story of my life.

I salute you!

PART 6: RUBIES OF LOVE

RUBIES OF LOVE

I asked a fellow traveler, "Why is a heart painted red?"
He said, "It's soft and vulnerable; it shows it has bled."
Then I asked an old lady, "Why is a heart painted red?"
"It's tough and old," she answered, "it's been stricken with dread."

"Why is a heart painted red?" I asked some friends.
They gave me different reasons, I couldn't comprehend.
A young man came along, he tried to answer;
"Red stands for passion, for romance, and fever."

I met a soldier, I asked him too.
He smiled at me and said he wished he knew.
"But let's have a coffee that will wake me up,
I've just come from battle, I need a pickup."
So we talked over coffee, cakes, and scones,
wondering why a heart is red, on shirts and tombstones?
"It's the color of blood, of losses, and gains;
it's the seat of emotions, of memories, and pain."

I thought over what he'd said and moved on,
then I met a child with a hand full of bonbons.
He was all of seven, his answer was the best;
he gave me a bonbon and took me to his nest.
We climbed up the tree, he showed me his treasure;
it was a little black bird with broken feathers.
The bird squeaked with joy and ate from his hand,
"I want him to get strong, and then fly to fairyland."

❊ ❊ ❊

❖ ❖ ❖

He said, "The heart is full of big, red cells.
It keeps you alive and tells if you are well."
His deed of love, his answer, both profound;
we held hands and walked, without a sound.

So let our hearts be red, full of life and vigor,
willing to serve and follow the Master.
Let's pursue a life full of faith, love, and peace,
for it is with the heart that one believes!

Here are three stories of my rubies of love.
May they inspire you to serve the One above.

CALLED TO LOVE

A deed of love is a powerful weapon in the hands of the right person. One deed can change two lives forever—the life of the one who initiates and the life of the one who receives. There are deeds of love that only you are enabled to do, through your unique circumstances. But it isn't easy. In loving others, we also enable them to exercise power over us. We open ourselves up for disappointments and pain. Therefore, many shy away from it. The Lord Jesus challenges us even further and calls us to love when we are not loved, to give when we do not receive, and to bless those who curse us.

One of the most powerful definitions of love that I have encountered is from a book called, *The Four Loves*, by C. S. Lewis. He said, "To love at all is to be vulnerable. Love anything and your heart will be wrung and possibly broken. If you want to make sure of keeping it intact you must give it to no one, not even an animal. Wrap it carefully round with hobbies and little luxuries; avoid all entanglements. Lock it up safe in the casket or coffin of your selfishness. But in that casket, safe, dark, motionless, airless, it will change. It will not be broken; it will become unbreakable, impenetrable, irredeemable. To love is to be vulnerable."[9]

We need to find the ocean of love: God is love. It is not an attitude or an attribute; it is God's nature. It is in God and through God that we are empowered to love. We are uniquely placed, each one in our corner of the planet; we are called to love those whom He has chosen and sent our way. They could be in the form of family member or friend, enemy or stranger, an urchin or a broken daughter of God, nothing is a coincidence. It is our privilege to love our neighbor, and in so doing we may learn to love God Himself.

---

[9] C. S. Lewis, The Four Loves (Great Britain: Harper Collins Publisher, 1952).

A COMPASSIONATE HEART

Freddy was crossing the street one morning. It was around 10:30 a.m., and he was on his way to the bazaar to buy some fresh fish. He loved buying fresh fish. It was as much about the fish as it was about the fisher folk. He took delight in talking to them, and he knew them by name. He knew their stories, and they appreciated his participation in their lives. Freddy loved being a part of someone else's story. He was seventy-two years old and a very popular man in his neighborhood, popular for his love and generosity. Freddy hadn't saved for his old age; in India, you mostly don't receive pension from the state. But that didn't stop him from sharing whatever he received from his daughters with those whom he felt were more in need.

Crossing streets in Mumbai is dangerous, especially if you are elderly. The relentless stream of traffic on the streets, the lack of zebra crossings,[10] and the hurried pace of life make this city extremely unfriendly toward the old and disabled. Freddy crossed the street and was meaning to step into a side alley that led to the fish market, but someone tapped him gently on his shoulder. It was an old man, perhaps in his sixties; he looked much older than his age. He was weak and frail. He had lost his way and needed to find a bus route to his destination. Freddy took a good look at the man who was sweating and seemed to be rather distraught. He held the man's hand gently and led him to a cup of tea. Much happened over that cup of tea. Freddy learned that the man had no money, and his family had written him off and neglected him. Freddy guided him to the bus stop and then on the spur of the moment, he hailed a taxi, ushered the old man in, and paid the taxi driver in advance to take him to his destination. It was a small amount but a huge act of love from a man who never had enough for his own tomorrow.

"I felt the old man's pain. He looked at me shocked when I put him in the taxi. He asked me why I was doing this. What could I say? I just smiled and shook his hand. He needed love, but a taxi fare is all that I could give him," Freddy narrated later on.

I believe Freddy gave the frail man much more. He gave him hope and a reason to believe that there was someone larger in our universe, someone who cared, a God Who had observed his pain and had sent him a rainbow of hope.

---

[10] crosswalks

TRUE GIVING IS SACRIFICIAL

Sheila lived in a large hutment[11] situated right outside the boundary walls of Freddy's apartment. She was a mother of three and terribly beaten and tortured by her drunkard husband who did nothing for his livelihood. He expected Sheila to work and fend for the family's needs, besides supplying him with money for his drunken charades. If she refused to obey, he would assault her and molest her. Sheila worked in Freddy's apartment and came in to work at 10:00 a.m. each morning. She spent a part of her day cleaning the apartment and helping Freddy with the house chores. His daughters had insisted that he hire her. Sheila had been looking out for a job close to home so she could keep an eye on her kids and earn some money as well. Freddy agreed to hire Sheila because he knew that she needed help right then.

It had been over a year since this arrangement had been put in place, and Sheila benefited hugely from Freddy's company. He taught her to cook inexpensive and tasty food for her children, she learned many household chores that she had not been good at, and Freddy shared breakfast and lunch with her each day. Sheila was as old as Freddy's daughter, and she found a father in him.

Sheila rang the doorbell an hour later than usual one morning. Freddy opened the door and gently led her in. Her demeanor clearly indicated that she had not slept all night, and some tragedy had taken place. Freddy made her a cup of tea and waited for her to speak. There had been heavy rains the night before. The streets of Mumbai had been flooded. Sheila's hutment had faced massive destruction and many homes were under water. A heavy storm had pierced its ferocious teeth into the meager belongings of the poor and ripped their lives apart. Sheila managed to convey between her sobs that the roof of her hut had been torn off with the heavy wind last night. Freddy worked at lightning speed. He knew that he had received some money from his daughter a couple of days ago. He went to the bank, withdrew it all, and spent the next days helping Sheila get the roof fixed.

---

[11] An encampment of huts

"I need to make a confession to you," he told his daughter one day. "You sent me some money for a rainy day; well, it happened literally. Sheila's home was destroyed with the rains, and I gave her the money to repair the roof of her house."

But Freddy had been ill, and the money sent to him by his daughter was for an emergency hospital visit, if needed. Freddy was a man who loved to love. He would not have hesitated for a moment in making the decision to give all he had so another person could have it all. What made Freddy love others as if they were his own? For these again were not mere acts of charity; they were deeds of love. He gave his love, his time, his money, and his prayers to the fellow travelers he met.

God's love comes to us in extraordinary ways. But it also comes in the form of ordinary things or those things that we take for granted on a daily basis. The fact that you received your food today is a sign of God's love. If you reached home safely after your day's obligations and were received by a happy, cheerful family, that is a sign of God's love for you today. If you received a love message or a call from an old friend after a decade, that is God's love being showered over you today.

Those who recognize that love and receive it daily are able to give, and they do it with that consciousness. These then are deeds of love, and they have the power to change lives. Every time we choose to give, we give to God Himself. In the book of Matthew, Jesus said that whatever we do to the least of our brothers we do unto Him (Matthew 25:40) — that we do unto God Himself! Every one of us has been made in the image of God. When we choose to love those who are ignored, vulnerable, and weak, we learn to love God, and we learn to open our hearts and receive from the very source of love — God Himself.

All I can claim to have learnt from the years I have spent in this world is that the only happiness is love, which is attained by giving, not receiving; and that the world itself only becomes the dear and habitable dwelling place it is when we who inhabit it know we are migrants, due when the time comes to fly away to other more commodious skies.

Malcolm Muggeridge, *Chronicles of Wasted Time*

MY FATHER

Freddy was my earthly father. He taught me his language of love. To love is to give, without conditions, without boundaries. He often said that you need a large heart to live on this planet, a heart that is as large and generous as the ocean.

His ability to give, without keeping a buffer for himself, was a supernatural gift. It was a gift that kept him alive and young, humorous and loving.

In 2004, as I struggled to settle down in a new country and make it my home, my father wrote a letter to me. In it he said, "Why do you worry when your father is still alive! I will always take care of you!" This from a man who was seventy-five years old then and had no material wealth, but he had the key to the biggest treasure box in the universe—the key to God's unlimited grace through Jesus Christ. He knew that his heavenly Father would provide, and God has. My heavenly Father is living; He has risen! I am being cared for, and I am deeply thankful!

Freddy's life here on earth was sprinkled with deeds of love that touched and helped people in distress and need. He was also my friend. I salute him!

JONATHAN'S JOURNEY FROM RAGE TO MERCY

Jonathan and Mariam moved to Delhi in 2009. They had lived in South Carolina for over thirty years, and this was their first big migration. They had been to India on a long stay for a couple of months many years ago, but nothing could have prepared them for this new venture. They planned to live in India for five years this time.

This vast country claims to have housed one of the oldest civilizations of the world, which had melted their hearts on their first stay. The dirt-smeared smiley faces of little children dressed in torn clothes, running around the streets begging for food or money, had broken their hearts each time. India was a warm country. They had made many friends during that long holiday, and some deep relationships were nurtured over the years. "India just grew on me. I didn't know that until it was time to leave," Jonathan said.

Mariam fell in love with the Himalayan ranges in the north of India. The wonderful times they had experienced in the Nubra Valley, walking on white masses of sand surrounded by the majestic Himalayas, were unforgettable moments. The people in Ladakh were discreet, yet warm and friendly at the same time. The cottages in the northeast with pretty curtains at the entrance and tiny patches of garden lined with various greens and tomatoes signified the humble dignity of the people staying behind those curtains. These people were not cast down by the constant rebellious forces that stopped the supply of basic necessities flowing into their towns. They had instead created their tiny patches of garden growing all they needed to survive. It had all been so endearing.

Jonathan and Mariam were well into the last week of their long holiday back then in November 2004. Friends and family at home in the United States were anxiously awaiting their return. But they had mixed feelings. Something had shifted so dramatically in their hearts. They had a compelling desire to stay, which they could not explain rationally, but neither could they discard it.

The farewell chai session at the tea stall in their neighborhood with their new friends was heartbreaking. Fifteen young street urchins gathered around a wooden bench. Some brought flowers and some gave pictures and paintings as farewell gifts. These children lived in a village opposite the guest house where Mariam and Jonathan had been staying. Over the months, they crossed each other's paths often, and what began as a shy wave of the hand blossomed into a beautiful friendship. A couple of hours passed by in happy jabbering at the farewell party, and it was time to finally head to the airport.

As they drove off in the old, white Ambassador to the airport, they vowed to come back someday and serve the poor in Delhi. Five years later, that moment came. They had worked toward that dream and here they were!

It took a few months for the couple to settle down in Delhi. Some of their friends helped them find a neat, spacious apartment in the southwest suburbs of Delhi. It was well connected with the mainstreams of life in the city—a self-sufficient suburb with schools, markets, houses of worship, and hospitals. Mariam and Jonathan felt blessed to have been able to rent this apartment at a fairly cheap rate. Housing in Delhi was expensive and this was indeed a miracle.

After many horrifying experiences with the public transport system in Delhi, they bought a car, thanks to the flow of financial support that came in from friends in the United States. They would have settled for a second-hand car, but they were warned by their Indian friends that things were not always the way they seemed, and there could be a few bad surprises a couple of days after they bought it. So Mariam and Jonathan chose a small Maruti Suzuki. It was the most popular car in the country and came in various models to suit most budgets.

It had been a week since the car purchase. The temperatures had risen; it was a stuffy afternoon. They had been driving for a good forty-five minutes on the streets of Delhi, where traffic rules don't really exist and signs and zebra crossings are never taken seriously. As Jonathan carefully navigated through the narrow lanes, swarmed with cattle and people, things suddenly moved into sixth gear! A tornado in the form of a mechanized rickshaw slammed into the back of their car. He could hear the dramatic sounds of screeching brakes and metal colliding against metal.

Everything seemed to be happening too fast. Jonathan wanted to slip out and check the damage, but he saw the rickshaw driver scoot and melt away into the thick traffic. He chased the rickshaw driver. It could well have been the Bollywood version of a James Bond movie. Jonathan finally caught up with the rickshaw.

Driving through the busy streets of Indian cities at any given hour is arduous. I have driven through the busy streets in Mumbai, Delhi, Bangalore, and other cities over many years myself. It is a miracle that you reach your destination with your sense of humor and patience intact.

Sensing an opportunity for a bribe, the traffic cops zoomed off behind the Maruti Suzuki on their motorbikes, like hungry sharks going in for the kill. In the meantime, Jonathan found himself embroiled in an argument with the rickshaw driver, who could not speak English. He fired away at the rickshaw driver, who by then was drenched in sweat and very nervous. He flung his hands helplessly in the air trying to justify his actions to an enraged Jonathan.

The cops arrived at the scene and joined in on the argument, which had now turned into a dramatic cacophony. Jonathan demanded that the rickshaw driver own up to his error and pay him for the damages done. The rickshaw driver helplessly pulled out his wallet and offered him all that he had; it was a torn fifty rupee bill. Jonathan was stumped. He had never had such an encounter before. What was he to do? He knew that his demands were justified, but on the other hand, before him stood a man who didn't even have a proper wallet. He took a good look at the rickshaw driver for the first time and as their eyes met, Jonathan was stirred with compassion. He knew beyond a reasonable doubt that this man was soaked in poverty. A kind of poverty, that Jonathan had never ever seen or experienced.

Closing his eyes for a moment, he sighed deeply. Various emotions intermingled within his being. He was speechless for a while. He found his rage transform into mercy rather instantly. There was an immense tautness in the air. A crowd had gathered around them. Everyone seemed involved, and passionate discussions filled the air. Jonathan opened up his wallet and offered the rickshaw driver two hundred rupee bills and said, "I would like you to have this money, not because you deserve it. You deserve to be behind bars. But I don't deserve all that I have been given either. God has been kind to me, and I offer His kindness now to you."

The passionate discussions ceased, and the gathering slowly dispersed. An emotional discomfort hung on between the two for a few moments. The rickshaw driver hesitantly folded his hands in thankfulness and went over to his rickshaw. Jonathan and Mariam made their way back to the car.

Whatever we do to the least of our brothers we also do unto Him indeed! Only here, Jonathan was compelled into sharing what he had already received.

The giving that comes out of receiving from God is of a different nature. It is a thankful giving. It is a giving that you do, fully knowing that you are actually just passing it on, passing on the blessings you have received from God to another. The joy in such giving comes from knowing that the Creator of the universe has abundant means of satisfying the needs and desires of His creation, but He chose to use you. God chose Jonathan to do this wonderful deed of love for a driver who had probably never received it in this manner. I salute you, Jonathan!

JESUS CAME VISITING
AT THE HOSPITAL

It was the autumn of 2011. Jess had comfortably perched herself on the hospital bed near a large window where she could watch the leaves fall. She was well prepared for this ordeal. Her mother underwent the same surgery twenty-three years ago and never came home. She had come to believe that her mother's fate was not hers, but that belief would now be tested. As the doctor gently pierced an empty needle under her skin, she felt alone. The needle stayed there all day! It was supposed to get her ready for the operation the next morning. But it did more than that. The constant irritation of something under her skin made her feel cold and vulnerable. These sensations transcended her physical realm and seeped deep into her soul.

There was something so powerful about physical pain. Jess had experienced physical pain before, and it had always made her vulnerable, not because of the physical symptoms as such, although they, of course, did matter, but it brought back various experiences of pain from her past. God had often used pain to heal her, and each experience had been a gigantic step of faith and freedom for her.

When you are in the throes of pain, you find yourself in a powerful grip and all your senses focus on the pain. It is a time when you are forced to live in the now. The day had moved pretty fast in the hospital. She had been admitted twenty-four hours before the surgery, and it turned out to be a day of several visits with doctors, nurses, and assistants asking various questions, constantly checking on her well-being. A counselor walked in mid-afternoon and Jess had an interesting talk with her. She was around sixty years old and soon the conversation took a different course. The counselor had meant to mentor Jess and help her get ready for the operation, but she began sharing her woes and aches with Jess instead. It seemed to be going all right that day until the visitations stopped and Jess confronted her first moment of total silence.

All she could feel and sense was the needle under her skin as if she were in a void. After all those years of prayers and building herself up, Jess realized that she had not yet surrendered this fear to God in totality. Yes, there might be a chance that she would face a similar fate as her mother—she might not wake up after this operation. She had no option now but to give in to whatever lay ahead. It was autumn and the days were short. The lights in the room sprang up, and Jess picked up her Bible and read, hoping for the time to pass faster than it did. She would be happy now to move into that state of oblivion, unconscious under the effects of strong anesthetics.

At around six in the evening, two visitors stepped into the room and greeted Jess. They were her new friends, Tim and Mary, people whom she never expected to see that day. She had met Tim and Mary during the summer at an outdoor event. They moved into her life during an emotionally exhausting time. Too many battles were going on and too many decisions had to be made; it was a phase of instability when Jess had no clue where things were going—everything had come undone. All the laces were untied and everything seemed haphazard. She had tried since then to live one day at a time.

The bright lights in the hospital room couldn't light up the darkness that Jess sensed within her. What was the matter? What had happened to her faith? She had prepared herself for this moment. If she would recover from this operation, there was a new adventure waiting to be lived. God had given her a peek into what was to come and yet, in that moment, sitting on the hospital bed, she felt numb.

Then God sent His angels to lift her, to encourage her, and to bless her. Tim and Mary walked in with huge smiles and hugged Jess. They had traveled a long distance to meet her that evening. There had been several obstacles on the journey. It had been a long one, but they were determined to be here at the hospital. They wanted to be a part of what Jess was undergoing.

Tim gave Jess a wooden placard that he had bought in Jerusalem, the city of Jesus. The placard read: "The Lord is my defense." He hung it over her bed. Jess' husband, Andy, joined them; the four of them held hands and Tim, Mary, and Andy prayed over Jess. It was magical.

Jess remembers, "As Tim and Mary entered my hospital room, my heart leapt with joy! You know that experience you had as a child, when your mom has left you at the neighbor's for a couple of hours and that deep sigh of pure joy on seeing her later again. Your childish instincts tell you that here before you stands the person who loves you the most! Tim and Mary did visit me, but my instincts and every fiber of my being knew that Jesus Himself had come to visit me. He need not have let me feel His presence so undeniably, but He did. Jesus visited me that night at the hospital."

Tim and Mary could have been doing many other things that evening. They were needed in many places. There were traffic jams and many reasons to turn back and head home that evening as they ventured to reach the hospital. But they were determined; it was an inner calling and they obeyed. They had no clue what this visit would mean for Jess, but they knew that they wanted to be there to meet her and to pray over her before the surgery.

God is indeed interested in our motives, and He enables us to act them out. Our actions can be amazing vessels of His grace toward others. They have the ability to let the supernatural mingle in our natural world, but we need to have the motive right.

Let your motive not be sympathy or obligation; let it be pure love. Jess recovered fabulously from her surgery. After that visit, Jess knew that she was safe in His hands, no matter where she would be after the operation, either in heaven with her Lord or here on earth.

As for Tim and Mary, they continue with their selfless deeds of love, working across continents, ministering to broken hearts, and serving the Lord as He leads them. I salute them!

GOD'S LANGUAGE OF LOVE

If I speak in the tongues of men or of angels, but do not have love,
I am only a resounding gong or a clanging cymbal.

If I have the gift of prophecy and can fathom all mysteries and all
knowledge, and if I have a faith that can move mountains,
but do not have love, I am nothing.

If I give all I possess to the poor and give over my body to hardship that I
may boast, but do not have love, I gain nothing.

Love is patient, love is kind. It does not envy,
it does not boast, it is not proud.
It does not dishonor others, it is not self-seeking, it is not easily angered,
it keeps no record of wrongs.
Love does not delight in evil but rejoices with the truth.
It always protects, always trusts, always hopes, always perseveres.
Love never fails.

But where there are prophecies, they will cease; where there are tongues,
they will be stilled; where there is knowledge,
it will pass away.
For we know in part and we prophesy in part, but when completeness
comes, what is in part disappears.

When I was a child, I talked like a child, I thought like a child, I rea-
soned like a child. When I became a man,
I put the ways of childhood behind me.

For now we see only a reflection as in a mirror;
then we shall see face to face. Now I know in part; then I shall know
fully, even as I am fully known.

And now these three remain: faith, hope and love.
But the greatest of these is love.

1 Corinthians: 13: 1–13

PART 7: MY TOURMALINES

MY TOURMALINES

Orange, red, yellow, and green,
indigo, violet, blue in between.
When you see these colors in the sky,
you clap your hands and leap with joy!

The rainbow is a symbol of hope,
so is friendship with true folk.
Some dear friends have held my hand,
from varied lands and cultures they span.

Each friend is a tourmaline,
unique and precious.
One cannot replace another;
they are simply priceless.

My friends have inspired me,
loved me, and encouraged me.
They've fed me and sheltered me
and gently corrected me.

But it isn't easy to find these gems;
many hurt you and are not friends.
The real ones stay and brighten your day;
the fake, they run when your sky is gray.

So be happy with the few genuine ones;
they will stand by you till your time is done.
Friends are God's gift to help us live,
to teach us to love, and generously give.

To challenge us, provoke us,
to dare us and bless us.
To inspire us, humor us,
to just be and cry with us.

I thank You, Lord, for my fellowship of friends.
Bless them and prosper them, let our love transcend.
Teach us to grow in unity and love,
to accept our differences as gifts from above.

To strengthen, to hold, to be your messenger of hope
when tragedy hits, and we are walking on tight ropes.
May we be Your hands, Your feet, Your heart,
Your vessels of love, till it's time to depart.

TO FRIENDSHIP

"In friendship, we think we have chosen our peers. In reality a few years' difference in the dates of our births, a few more miles between certain houses, the choice of one university instead of another . . . the accident of a topic being raised or not raised at a first meeting — any of these chances might have kept us apart. But, for a Christian, there are, strictly speaking no chances. A secret master of ceremonies has been at work. Christ, who said to the disciples, 'Ye have not chosen me, but I have chosen you,' can truly say to every group of Christian friends, 'Ye have not chosen one another but I have chosen you for one another.' The friendship is not a reward for our discriminating and good taste in finding one another out. It is the instrument by which God reveals to each of us the beauties of others."[12]

C. S. Lewis, *The Four Loves*

I cannot end this book without saluting all the tourmalines that God has given me in the form of some very special women and men, whom I know as my dear friends.

Indeed, like the different colors, texture, composition, and form of tourmalines, my friends are each unique and notable. I could not have chosen them myself. Yes, as C. S. Lewis said, friendship is not a reward for my discriminating taste and ability to find it. If it were so, then I would have ended up with no friends at all!

My friends have walked into my life from different continents, at various times and seasons, and they are here to stay. Friends love at all times, no matter where they are placed on earth. My friends have counseled me and loved me, they have advised me and stood by me in times of adversity. And

---

[12] C. S. Lewis, *The Four Loves* (Great Britain: Harper Collins Publisher, 1952).

they have let me be a part of their journey too, accepting what I have to offer. The Bible says, "As iron sharpens iron, so one person sharpens another" (Proverbs 27:17). I have the privilege of experiencing it each day. Thank You, dear Lord, for choosing my friends for me and me for them.

PART 8: A TRIBUTE TO MARRIAGE

Excerpts from a wedding sermon by Dietrich Bonhoeffer[13]

It is right and proper for a bride and bridegroom to welcome and celebrate their wedding day with a unique sense of triumph. When all the difficulties, obstacles, hindrances, doubts, and misgivings have been, not made light of, but honestly faced and overcome—and it is certainly better not to take everything for granted—then both parties have indeed achieved the most important triumph of their lives. With the 'Yes' that they have said to each other, they have by their free choice given a new direction to their lives; they have cheerfully and confidently defied all the uncertainties and hesitations with which, as they know, a lifelong partnership between two people is faced; and by their own free and responsible action they have conquered a new land to live in.

Every wedding must be an occasion of joy that human beings can do such great things, that they have been given such immense freedom and power to take the helm in their life's journey. The children of the earth are rightly proud of being allowed to take a hand in shaping their own destinies, and something of this pride must contribute to the happiness of a bride and bridegroom. We ought not to be in too much of a hurry here to speak piously of God's will and guidance. It is obvious, and it should not be ignored, that it is your own very human wills that are at work here, celebrating their triumph; the course that you are taking at the outset is one that you have chosen for yourselves; what you have done and are doing is not in the first place, something religious, but something quite secular. So you yourselves, and you alone, bear the responsibility for what no one can take from you.

Unless you can boldly say today: 'That is our resolve, our love, our way,' you are taking refuge in false piety. 'Iron and steel may pass away, but our love shall abide forever.' That desire for earthly bliss, which you want to find in one another, and in which to quote the medieval song, one is the comfort of

***

[13] Excerpts from Lutheran wedding, "A wedding sermon by Dietrich Bonhoeffer," 1943, accessed July 2014, http://lutheranweddings. blogspot.in/search?q=it+is+right+and+proper.

the other both in body and in soul — that desire is justified before God and man.

Everyone has wished you well, and now it has been given to you to find each other and to reach the goal of your desires. You yourselves know that no one can create and assume such a life from his own strength, but that what is given to one is withheld from another; and that is what we call God's guidance. So today, however much you rejoice that you have reached your goal, you will be just as thankful that God's will and God's way have brought you here; and however confidently you accept responsibility for your action today, you may and will put it today with equal confidence into God's hands.

As God today adds His 'Yes' to your 'Yes,' as He confirms your will with His will, and as He allows you, and approves of, your triumph and rejoicing and pride, He makes you at the same time instruments of His will and purpose both for yourselves and for others. In His unfathomable condescension God does add His 'Yes' to yours; but by doing so, He creates out of your love something quite new — the holy estate of matrimony.

Your love is your own private possession, but marriage is more than something personal — it is a status, an office. Just as it is the crown, and not merely the will to rule, that makes the king, so it is marriage, and not merely your love for each other, that joins you together in the sight of God and man.

As high as God is above man, so high are the sanctity, the rights, and the promise of marriage above the sanctity, the rights, and the promise of love. It is not your love that sustains the marriage, but from now on, the marriage that sustains your love.

It is a blessed thing to know that no power on earth, no temptation, no human frailty can dissolve what God holds together; indeed, anyone who knows that may say confidently: What God has joined together, can no man put asunder. Free from all anxiety that is always a characteristic of love, you can now say to each other with complete and confident assurance: We can never lose each other now; by the will of God we belong to each other till death.

God gives you Christ as the foundation of your marriage. 'Welcome one another, therefore, as Christ has welcomed you, for the glory of God' (Romans 15:7). In a word, live together in the forgiveness of your sins, for without it no human fellowship, least of all a marriage, can survive. Don't insist on your rights, don't blame each other, don't judge or condemn each other, don't fault with each other, but accept each other as you are, and forgive each other every day from the bottom of your hearts.

From the first day of your wedding till the last the rule must be: 'Welcome one another . . . for the glory of God.'

That is God's word for your marriage. Thank Him for it; thank Him for leading you thus far; ask Him to establish your marriage, to confirm it, sanctify it, and preserve it. So your marriage will be 'for the praise of His glory.' Amen.

A CORD OF THREE

"Two are better than one,
because they have a good return for their labor:
If either of them falls down,
one can help the other up.
But pity anyone who falls and has no one to help them up.

Also, if two lie down together,
they will keep warm.
But how can one keep warm alone?

Though one may be overpowered,
two can defend themselves.
A cord of three strands is not quickly broken."

Ecclesiastes 4:9–12

I cannot thank you enough, Andreas, for making so much possible.

Thank You, Jesus, You indeed are the key strand that holds, nourishes, and strengthens our cord.

FOR ANDREAS

It was a still night,
my hero lost the fight.
He sat at the goal post,
like a lost knight.
It was just a game, but his sadness touched my heart.
One wins, the other loses, does it have to be so hard?

Then I met a friendly you,
you were for the winners.
Your prayer got its due;
my team was the losers.
Out of joy and sadness, a new bond was built.
Shoulders were leaned on, there was sharing to the hilt.

Dreams and songs crossed continents,
each evening was engaging.
We talked of sports and elephants,
much was in the planning.
The distance soon began to hurt, no spaceship was on hire.
The oceans and the mountains, they heard our desires.

Then one fine day in Feb,
we took our vows at the shore.
I packed my bags with chili and rice,
made you my home for evermore.
Together you and I, we have traveled across shores,
God has held our hands; He has loved us and restored.

Thanks, dear man, for your patience and wit,
you have been challenged, I have seen your grit.
My heart sings along, this song is just for you.
I only want to do everything with you!
Together with you, I want to grow old.
Holding your hand, I want to stroll.

And when the shadows fall and the risen Son calls,
we will find each other there, in heaven's great halls.

THE CLOUDS

The heavens are full of His glory
and He has placed His gems below.
We gaze and gaze at the stars and the planets,
the sky so rich, the clouds cotton blankets.

And if you watch these clouds carefully,
a game they play, sometimes gray, at times blue belly.
A jelly bean mixed with lavender pink,
it's not just the colors, I see faces and kings.

You may never have thought much of these clouds before.
I tell you they are precious; they bring the stars to the fore.
Bland would be the sky and the stars not so pretty,
if the clouds wouldn't dress them and serenade their beauty.

❊ ❊ ❊

*** *** ***

So I urge you to gaze and look out for those clouds;
they tell you stories with pictures and sound.
It's a sky full of life; there are warriors and horses,
bookstores and candy jars and lots of golf courses.

Houses made of gems and precious stones,
their chimneys spew smoke in colorful tones.
Children are eating hot puddings and pies,
the women all dressed to watch the moonrise.

Tigers and lions laze in fields of daffodils,
birch trees and oaks all doing their drills.
The grass below thick and lush, they are rolling down the slope;
there is singing and laughter, someone's cracking a joke.

Snowy white eagles glide with parrots on their wings.
Warm, golden mountains with the colors of spring.
Oh, there's a lot going on in the clouds up there;
keep gazing and watching and be prepared.

You may even see the Knight in His shining armor;
yes, He lives and He is coming —
let's be ready and not stammer!
What will you tell Him when He stretches out His hand
and His glance will jolt you right where you stand?

Dedicated to Andreas:
Thank you for being my mate, my very best friend.

A SONG TO SING ALONG!

YOU MET ME

You met me that night at the bus stop;
my toes were frosty, my life was a knot.
You carried me home and calmed all my fears,
You whispered shalom and wiped all my tears.

Refrain
You said I'm chosen, a Priesthood I belong
and I sang again, as I strode along.

You met me that noon at the shopping mall
where she abused me, made me feel so small.
You reminded me You're my Creator.
You've woven my skin and given it color.

❈ ❈ ❈

✤ ✤ ✤

Refrain
You said I'm chosen, a Priesthood I belong
and I sang again, as I strode along.

You met me that morning in the sunny room,
me sitting on the couch with coffee and doom.
I did not know what tomorrow would bring,
a surgery, a rift, I was driven to the brink.

Refrain
You said I'm chosen, a Priesthood I belong
and I sang again, as I strode along.

You met me at the chemist, words of love You spoke,
as Grandma stretched her hand asking for a smoke.
She got no cigarette, a smile and hug instead.
Up the hill she went with flowers in her head.

Refrain
You said I'm chosen, a Priesthood I belong
and I sang again, as I strode along.

Oh, how can I forget, the huge eagle You sent?
Perched on a pipe, he watched over our event.
You still my restless heart, oh how much You care.
You meet me all the time; You are always there!

Refrain
You said I'm chosen, a Priesthood I belong
and I sang again, as I strode along.

Please do visit my website: jenniferriegler.com for a free download of the song "You Met Me."
I would love to welcome you there and get to know you!

ACKNOWLEDGMENTS

Quicksand has many champions, angels, fairy godmothers, and a whole ship of friends! I thank them. But above all, I have to thank my Creator Who is the air that I breathe. Without Him, I would not have written this book to its end. He has been patting me ever so gently on my knuckles, being the voice of my conscience, inspiring me to stay authentic and persevere on many bad weather days.

I want to begin by thanking my mother, my father, and all my writing teachers in school at St. Mary's Convent in Mumbai. Without their assiduousness and persistence, I would not have cultivated an obsession for the English language and its amazing ability to empower you with words, so you may express your deepest thoughts and dreams, your nightmares and fears, your hopes and tragedies, your past and future and, of course, your very present.

The illustrations in *Quicksand* are Aditya Jhunjhunwala's contributions. Thank you Aditya! It has been an unforgettable journey working together with you. I thank Deepak Peters for working together with me on the book cover. You enhanced my simple imagination and converted it into a beautiful book cover! I would also like to thank Patricia Foster for her valuable contribution to the editing process.

I have to thank a few special people without whom *Quicksand* would not have seen the light of day. They are named here in no particular order, and each one has equally contributed to the making of this book.

Thank you, dear people, for being a part of my journey: Sujatha Iyer, Janet Raymond, Rebecca Raymond, Sanjiv Antao, Mehboob Ghai, Rachel Zuch, Karin Ebert, Wolfgang Ebert, Kristy North, Mal North, Beresford Job, Belinda Job, Solomon Missal, Sunitha Missal, Perola Menon, Bertha Roman, Vijaya Tamhane, Nathalie Karam, Ralph Crasto, Tim Tiner, Mary Lou Tiner, Bhupen Gosai, Ralph Francis, Gayle Francis, Michael Spacil, Andreas Riegler, Darya Crockett and the team at Innovo Publishing.

FOR REBECCA

Dear Rebecca,

One of the greatest joys that I have ever received is you. Carrying you in my arms, when you were just a few hours old on our earth, was an overwhelming experience. It has been my privilege to see you grow. I hope that one day you will read this book. I dedicate the stories of your grandma and grandpa to you! You did not get to meet them personally, but I hope you will meet them in the pages of *Quicksand* and that it will give you joy.

Your loving aunty, Jennifer

Film quotations are taken from the following sources:

American Beauty, www.imbd.com, date of access: January 17, 2013, Year of production: 1999, Director Sam Mendes.

The Legend of Bagger Vance, Year of production: 2000, Director: Robert Redford.

Memoirs of a Geisha, Year of production: 2005, Director: Rob Marshall.

Pretty Woman, Year of production: 1990, Director: Garry Marshall.

Star Wars, Episode V, Year of production: 1980, Director: Irvin Kershner.

CPSIA information can be obtained at www.ICGtesting.com
Printed in the USA
BVOW08s0937211015

423449BV00002B/105/P